CHURCH WEALTH AND BUSINESS INCOME

By the same author:

MILTON AND SERVETUS, A Theological Interpretation

THE MODERNITY OF MILTON

THE THEORY OF LOGICAL EXPRESSION

PLASTER SAINT

THE RELIGION OF THE OCCIDENT

CHURCH WEALTH AND BUSINESS INCOME

by

MARTIN A. LARSON

Philosophical Library
New York

ACKNOWLEDGMENT

The research on which this work is based was done at the request and through the cooperation of Protestants and Other Americans United for Separation of Church and State. Special appreciation is due to Dr. Glenn Archer and Dr. C. Stanley Lowell for their help and encouragement, without which this book could not have been written.

"The . . . assets and real estate holdings" of the Catholic Church "must exceed those of Standard Oil, A. T. & T., and U.S. Steel combined."

> Quoted from:
> Father Richard Grider
> in THE WALL STREET
> JOURNAL

*

"Earnings from businesses that have no direct connection with the religious purpose of the church should pay income taxes, regardless of how that income is used; the basic criterion should be the source from which the income is derived, rather than the use to which it is put."

> Quoted from:
> The Baptist Joint Committee on
> Public Affairs
> in CHRISTIANITY TODAY

*

The rapidly growing tax-exemptions "may present the state with problems of such magnitude that their only solution will be the revolutionary expropriation of church properties."

> Quoted from:
> Dr. Eugene Carson Blake
> in FACT

*

Error #55 is that "The Church must be separated from the State and the State from the Church."

> Quoted from:
> Pope Pius IX
> in the Encyclical, THE
> SYLLABUS OF ERRORS,
> which was promulgated on
> December 8, 1864

TABLE OF CONTENTS

FOREWORD

The purpose of this study is to investigate the extent of tax-exempt property in the United States and to determine how much of this is owned by religious organizations, what unrelated business income these receive, and in what proportions such real estate and revenues are divided among the principal denominations. For the sake of convenience, throughout this study, Buddhist, Swedenborgian, Islamite, Divine Science, New Thought, Eastern Rite, Polish National Catholic congregations, etc., all of which are independent and contribute to our religiously pluralistic society, are included under the heading, "Protestants, Etc."

We also summarize the comparative historical development which has taken place within the principal American religious groups; and explain the federal income tax laws and regulations, as they apply to churches and other exempt entities and as they relate to the separation of church and state.

The problem caused by the ever-increasing proportion of exempt property is now widely recognized. In 1931, only 12% of all real estate in this country was immune from local taxation; by 1961, this ratio had risen to 30%,[1] and it is growing apace. Those who must carry the increasing load are crying for relief.

No similar study has been made for many years. It is true that elaborate censuses of religious bodies were taken by the federal government in 1906, 1916, 1926, and 1936; but even these excluded many types of denominational holdings, such as colleges, seminaries, hospitals, cemeteries, publishing houses, commercial investments, etc. So far as we know, then, this is the first attempt, based upon actual records, ever made in this country to determine the total extent of church wealth.

A complete census of religious property is impossible, first, because of the magnitude of the task; second, because no one has the authority to demand the necessary information; third, because, in a great many communities, church and other exempt properties carry no assessments on the tax-rolls; and, fourth, because what is called the "Unrelated Business Income" of churches is very often a top-secret, into which no level of government or any one else may pry and which, therefore, remains in a state of general concealment.

In spite of these difficulties, it is, nevertheless, possible to describe a number of representative church-held commercial investments; and, by choosing certain key and representative communities, to determine the exact assessments and the approximate value of religiously used properties in a substantial and representative segment of the American economy. Then, by extrapolating the result, it is possible to estimate the investment in visible church property in the United States.

In choosing communities for analysis, two considerations took precedence: first, whether the city was representative of the country as a whole or a substantial portion of it; and, second, whether reliable information was available. Several cities which had been under consideration had to be abandoned because their tax records carry no assessments for exempt properties; others were rejected because they were not typical.

For various reasons, Buffalo, Washington, Baltimore, and Denver were finally selected for analysis. Buffalo is similar to many large cities, such as Boston, Newark, Paterson, Providence, Cleveland, Detroit, Chicago, St. Louis, San Francisco, and New Orleans, where Catholics became by far the largest communion nearly a century ago and have always so remained. The District of Columbia constitutes a national melting pot, where every creed and organization is represented. Baltimore is a trading and manufacturing city, southern in flavor, yet dependent for its economic strength upon its northern commerce. Although it was the first Catholic stronghold in this country, it is today by no means a Catholic city. Finally, Denver was chosen because it is a classic representative of a predominantly Protestant-secular culture, in which the Catholic Church has expanded and prospered.

TABLES I and II (Appendix) show a 1964 population of 2,722,000 in these four cities, of whom 147,200, or 5.41%, were Jewish; 570,500, or 20.95%, Catholic; 735,800, or 27.03%, Protestant, etc.; and 1,268,800 or 46.61%, without specific church affiliation. Since the large cities tend to be less religious than the suburbs or the countryside, we find a ratio of 53.39% of church communicants in the former compared to 63.41% in the nation as a whole. In a population of 186,000,000 in 1963-64, we had a reported total of 5,509,000 Jews; 43,847,938 Catholics; and 68,598,064 Protestants, etc. The Jews, according to these statistics, made up 2.96% of the population; the Catholics 23.57%; and the Protestants, etc., 36.88%. This left 68,045,000, or 36.59%, which, although this total includes a great many Protestant children, still must leave at least 50,000,000 who may be classified as unchurched.

We should add that although the proportion of Jews and Negroes is considerably higher in these four cities than in the nation as a whole, the Catholic-Protestant proportion there is very nearly the same as in the whole country.

It is true that the District of Columbia has two important Catholic universities, which give it a top-heavy investment in this field. It has also the Episcopal National Cathedral and the magnificent Shrine of the Immaculate Conception (which we exclude from our base in estimating national religious property, since these are not local in scope). It is further true that the proportion of Catholic school enrollment is slightly higher in these cities than in the nation for the reason that this denomination has not yet been able to construct parochial schools in the suburbs and the countryside to serve all the youth of its faith. It is also true that in 1936 the religious wealth of the four cities was more than 3% of the national total, which gave them an almost double per capita ratio.

We have concluded, nevertheless, for reasons to be elaborated in Chapter VI, that the per capita value of church property in our pilot cities, both Catholic and Protestant, in comparison with the national, has now declined so sharply that it very nearly approximates that in the United States as a whole; and this is true partly because of the great increase of Negroes in them since 1936. For while this race comprises only 10 or 11% of the national population, it makes up fully 30% in our four cities; and, although Negroes are very religious and have many churches, these generally involve much smaller investments than the average. This Negro increase has also sharply reduced the ratio of Catholic communicants among city church affiliates and has increased the Protestant proportion even more, since Negroes are overwhelmingly of this faith and do not easily convert to Catholicism, partly because of the cost of sending their numerous offspring to parochial schools. In 1950, 10,892,694 American Negroes, or 75% of all the members of this race, were communicants in the Baptist and Methodist denominations alone.[2] Protestants have therefore increased in our four cities, even in the face of a declining population, but their total wealth has declined. And this is one of the causes why per capita church wealth in the four cities, as a base from which to estimate the national, may now be too small rather than too large.

Our research in these cities included a complete transcription and analysis of all items of privately owned tax-exempt property carried on the assessment rolls. The totals so obtained were checked against those officially published; and each reorganization of this material is based upon our own transcription.

INTRODUCTION

The history of mankind is a constantly flowing stream, in which the waters of one age irrigate and fructify the next; we are part and parcel of our past; and this is particularly true of the origin, development, and diversification of Christianity. The informed student can scarcely fail to recognize the remarkable parallel between the comparative growth of the various denominations in the United States during the last two hundred and fifty years and the comparable process which occurred in the Graeco-Roman world between 50 and 300 A.D. This country was founded, built, and established almost exclusively by a great variety of Protestants and secularists; only at a later date and, for a long time in very small numbers, did the Catholic Church achieve any substantial expansion and development in the United States. However, its growth in communicants, wealth, and influence during the last 150 years is perhaps the most extraordinary phenomenon which has occurred upon the American continent.

Before the end of the first century of our era, there already existed a remarkable number of independent Christian communions; and in the second, these and many new ones proliferated over the Roman Empire in astonishing variety. Some of these were empire-wide in scope and had their own canons of sacred literature. The movement which culminated in Catholic Christianity, led by a number of extremely able men, had its beginnings early in the second century. These practical clerics differed from other Christian teachers and organizers in that they (1) envisioned a universal church; and (2) believed that the ecclesiastical polity should be united with the civil government. In the course of time, these leaders assumed episcopal authority

xiii

and met in councils designed to unify their organization, doctrines, and practices.

As the ancient Catholic Church grew in power and influence, it came into severe conflict with the Roman authorities. For leading raids upon pagan shrines and altars, St. Cyprian of Carthage was beheaded in 258. In the year 303, the Emperor Diocletian embarked upon a course of persecution during which, according to Edward Gibbon, about 2,000 bishops and other leading Catholics were executed. His successor, Constantine, however, who became a Christian convert, issued his Edict of Toleration at Milan in 313, under which all religions were made equal, and free to worship at their pleasure. Nevertheless, in 325, the same emperor began issuing a long series of rescripts under which not only the pagan cults but all deviationist forms of Christianity also were proscribed under the severest penalties.

The results of this union of church and state, in which the latter was no more than a servant, were soon reflected in the pursuant imperial decrees. The dominant clergy were placed on the public payroll; they were exempted from military duty and from all personal or collective taxation; and they were given immunity from all prosecution in the civil courts. The church was empowered to receive gifts and legacies; the estates of all persons who died without direct heirs were conferred upon the church; its old edifices were repaired or rebuilt and many new ones constructed at public expense. Catholic Christians only were permitted to hold public office. The church grew in wealth and political power in Europe until it owned at least one-third of all property (which was tax-free) and dominated almost every government. The social and political system established under Constantine continued as the prevailing form for more than a thousand years, a period known as the Dark or the Middle Ages.

When the American founding fathers established this nation, it was against the background of strife, bloodshed, and desolation which had for centuries been the common lot of Europeans, groaning under the slavery of a church-state union controlled by an authoritarian theocracy. Those who wrote our constitution believed that freedom, human dignity, and progress are possible only when the civil government is unencumbered by church commitments or alliances and when the religious convictions of each citizen remain his own private concern. These men, led by Jefferson, Madison, Washington, Paine, Franklin, and others, knew what they were about and intended that in this land the state should remain forever secular; that it would be separated completely from every church, and that each and every human being should have the right to worship as he pleased, or not at all, and that never, never would any one be required or permitted to contribute directly or indirectly to any church through the government. Religion, they were convinced, must be free, voluntary, and divorced from the civil power.

It was possible to establish such a government in the United States because—whether the various denominations believed in church-state separation or not—not one of the many Protestant groups was strong enough to enforce its will upon the rest. Each could therefore best protect itself by giving political power or preference to none. And thus was established the first major commonwealth in the world since Diocletian in which it was the purpose of the ruling power to keep church and state entirely apart.

The First Amendment to our Constitution declares that "Congress shall make no law respecting an establishment of religion or prohibiting the free exercise thereof . . ." This means simply and categorically that any law which has relevance to the existence, activities, or financial status of any religious group or ideology is forbidden. This being true, it is certain that many unconstitutional laws have been passed and are now being enforced in the United States.

Part One:

CHURCHES AND THEIR EXEMPT REAL ESTATE

CHAPTER I:

DENOMINATIONAL GROWTH
IN THE UNITED STATES

Colonial churches. The English colonists who settled at James-town, Virginia, in 1607 came in search of wealth rather than liberty; but the Puritans who landed at Plymouth in 1620 were interested primarily in religious freedom, as were the Quakers and many others who followed in ever-increasing streams. Within a short time, we find Baptist, Dutch Reformed, Lutheran, Presbyterian, Jewish, and Roman Catholic congregations; and by 1750 there were 250 societies of Friends, exceeded in number by only the Anglicans and the Congregationalists.

The slow Catholic growth. Spanish Catholics founded Santa Fe, New Mexico, in 1540. The oldest official congregation of that faith in the New World was established by the French at St. Augustine, Florida, in 1565; and the first who settled in the original colonies arrived from Ireland in 1634 and established themselves in Maryland.[1]

For more than two hundred years, Catholics continued to be a very small minority. Even in 1696, there were still only seven Catholic families in New York; and as late as 1775, their descendants had to journey to Philadelphia to receive the sacraments.[2] In 1785, in a colonial population of 3,600,000 (cf. TABLE V), there were only 18,200 Catholics, of whom 15,000 were in Maryland, 1,500 in New York, 700 in Pennsylvania, and 200 in Virginia.[3]

In order to qualify for public office under the Continental Congress, every American was required to renounce all foreign jurisdiction, whether political or religious; it was therefore necessary for Catholics to devise a plan by which an ecclesiastical superior might be appointed "in such a way as to retain absolutely the spiritual jurisdiction of the Holy See and at the same time remove all ground for objecting to us as though we held anything hostile to the national independence."[4]

In 1785, a group of Catholic families in the city of New York organized as an independent congregation, purchased a church site owned by a board of trustees, and set out to hire a pastor of their own preference. The Jesuit priest, Bishop John Carroll, who founded Georgetown University in Washington, D. C., denounced the New York communicants in the strongest terms, saying that their act "would result in the formation of distinct and independent societies in nearly the same manner as the Congregational Presbyterians." Several churches, declares an official Catholic publication, "for a time firmly resisted the authority of the bishops"[5] in this regard; and it was many years before the last Catholic congregation in the United States surrendered its property to its bishop.

By 1790, the original colonies had grown to sixteen states with a population of 3,929,214; and in 1810, this number had risen to 7,239,881,[6] with still only approximately 150,000 Catholics,[7] a total which, even so, represented a quadrupled proportionate increase in twenty years. As late as 1840, the United States was still overwhelmingly Protestant or secular.

The flood. Soon after, however, the Catholic tidal wave began to arrive. Because of the abortive revolution of 1848 in Germany, 2,467,317 predominantly Catholic immigrants arrived from that country between 1850 and 1870. And, largely because of the potato famine of 1845-50 in Ireland, 1,694,830 immigrants from that country came to the United States between 1841 and 1860,[8] most of whom settled in the large cities. Their descendants to this day supply most of the members of the Catholic hierarchy in the United States.

Following 1845, therefore, the complexion of American society underwent a rapid and drastic change. A mere handful of Catholic churches suddenly became hundreds and then thousands; communicants, once numbered in thousands, were reckoned by millions; and they became a colossal political force, widely

4

feared and to combat which the Know-Nothing Party came into existence about 1860.

Religion in the public schools. It is interesting to note that when public schools were first established in this country, Catholics insisted on the complete elimination of religious instruction in them; and this position was made official by the Second Provincial Council held in Baltimore in 1840. Protestants were then the vast majority and most of them wanted their children taught Calvinist doctrine and theology; but "The Catholics," we read in the *Yearbook of 1928,* "objected to conditions which constrained their children to attend, or take part in, non-Catholic services or instruction. The Catholics initiated and developed the parochial school system in order to meet the demands of conscience and the right of the parent to secure the religious education which he wished for his child." [9]

The denominational growth. TABLE III (Appendix) shows the comparative growth in the number of church organizations from 1660 to 1950. At the former date, there were seven denominations in the colonies with 154 congregations, of which 12 were Catholic, 75 Congregational, 41 Anglican, 13 Dutch Reformed, 5 Presbyterian, 4 Baptist, and 4 Lutheran. In 1860, there were 52,532 congregations, among which the Methodists, with 19,883, had achieved preponderance and of which 2,550 were Roman Catholic, 12,150 Baptist, 6,406 Presbyterian, and 728 Quaker. Ninety years later, in 1950, there were 15,533 Catholic parish churches and more than eighty Protestant denominations with some 200 bodies and something like 240,000 congregations. TABLE IV (Appendix), based on reports for 1963, shows that there were then 98[10] denominations in the country with 252 bodies, of which 222 were Protestant with 64,929,941 members. The Roman Catholics had 23,412 churches, 17,445 parishes, and 43,847,938 members.[11] The Baptists had emerged as the largest Protestant denomination with twenty-two divisions, 92,362 congregations, and nearly 20,000,000 inclusive members.

These tables also reveal that the Lutherans, Methodists, and Baptists experienced a spectacular growth between 1820 and 1950; that others, like the Disciples, Presbyterians, Quakers, Unitarians, and Universalists declined after 1900; and that a whole galaxy of new ones came into existence, especially the

5

Mormons, Christian Scientists, New Thought groups, and a variety of apocalyptic and pentecostal congregations. Protestant churches and communicants increased sharply between 1950 and 1964; the most salient fact, however, was the constant and extraordinary expansion of the Roman Catholic Church which had gone on for many decades. TABLE V (Appendix) shows that in 1785, its communicants made up one half of one per cent of the population and 1.5% of the religious affiliates; in 1890, these percentages had grown to 13.25 and 30.4% respectively; TABLE XXXI (Appendix) indicates that by 1936 these had increased to 15.53 and 35.68%; and in 1964 to 23.57 and 37.16%. In less than one hundred and eighty years, Roman Catholics increased in number from 18,200 to almost 45,000,000, as shown in TABLE VI (Appendix).

In addition, the Catholics in the United States have a vast network of institutions paralleling nearly all those which exist in secular society: there is no phase of life which is not dominated by some church activity. Protestants, on the other hand, meet in their churches on Sunday and then utilize the public schools and countless other facilities in common. The development of Catholicism in the United States may be traced in its annual official directories, published since 1817. TABLE VI shows how this activity expanded between 1891 and 1964. While the population of the country was increasing from 62,900,000 to 186,000,000 or 197%, the Protestant communicants from 14,220,000 to 64,929,941, or 357%, the Catholics increased from 8,579,966 to 44,847,371, or 423%.

Such statistics, however, tell only a fraction of the story. For, in addition to their churches, chapels, and missions, the Catholics had, by 1963-4, 571 seminaries, with 48,750 students training for the priesthood; 296 colleges and universities, with 366,172 students; 2,458 high schools, with 1,068,541 pupils; and 10,902 parochial and other elementary schools, with a full-time enrollment of 4,556,616. Furthermore, they gave religious instruction to 4,316,931 pupils attending public schools on released time. They had also a vast chain of cemeteries, convents, monasteries, hospitals, newspapers, magazines, and orphanages. Besides these, the hierarchy has enormous intangible and commercial holdings, which we will consider in PART TWO.

6

Catholic immigrants. Between 1830 and 1920 the great Catholic accretions came from immigration, which was several times greater from Catholic than from Protestant countries. Of the 29,675,138 persons who arrived from Europe during this period, 22,962,194 came from wholly or predominantly Catholic countries, leaving only some seven millions from the Scandinavias, England, Scotland, Switzerland, Turkey, and Holland. The first heavy influx of Catholics, as we have noted, came from Ireland and Germany. The largest subsequent waves came from Austria-Hungary, Russia, Poland, and Italy, which supplied 8,716,272 out of a total of 12,512,580 who arrived from Europe between 1901 and 1920.[12] The Catholic Church must have lost a large proportion of its European arrivals; otherwise it would have had many more than 12,651,944 members in 1906, 16,309,310 in 1915, or 18,654,028 in 1925.[13] Had these and their offspring all continued in their old-world faith, this would long since have become a Catholic nation.

Growth without immigration. The amazing fact is, therefore, that even though immigration from Catholic countries to the United States came to a virtual standstill after 1924,[14] the Catholic Church expanded enormously, especially after 1936. During the twenty-eight years following that date, as shown in TABLE VI, its seminarians increased by nearly 26,000, or 113%; its college and university enrollment by 264,000, or 250%; its secondary and elementary school attendance by 3,106,000, or 119%; and its baptisms by 653,300, or 82%. While the population of the country was increasing from 128,000,000 to 186,000,000, or 45%, the number of Catholic communicants increased from 20,735,000 to 44,847,000, or 116%. It was during this period also that religious instruction under released time for Catholic youth in the public schools was inaugurated, a program which now involves about five millions.

TABLE VII (Appendix) shows the comparative growth in the wealth of American churches between 1850 and 1936. The central fact reflected here is the steady and progressive increase in the value of Catholic property, especially in comparison with the Protestant. As late as 1850, when heavy streams of Irish and German immigrants had already arrived, their churches and rectories were reported to be worth $9,256,758 and constituted only

7

10.54% of the total of such properties, which was $87,328,807; by 1936, reported Catholic religious wealth had increased to $891,435,725 and comprised 23.73% of the total. Meanwhile, the Protestant ratio dropped from 89 to 72.98%.

By 1890, the Catholics had become the most numerous single communion with 6,257,871 members, but not as yet the richest. The Methodists with 4,589,284 members then owned church property worth $132,140,179, against $118,371,366[15] invested in Catholic churches and rectories. By 1906, however, the Catholics had outdistanced all rivals in this respect also, with $292,638,787, compared to $229,450,996 of Methodist and $150,189,446[16] of Presbyterian property. The Baptists, Episcopalians, Lutherans, and Congregationalists were by this time far behind; and all other denominations were, by comparison, poor indeed.

It is also notable that Catholic churches have always been by far the largest and that their growth has been much more rapid: the average Protestant congregation had 107 members in 1890;[17] 176 in 1936;[18] and 226 in 1964.[19] Catholic churches averaged 1,125 members in 1891, 1,565 in 1936, and 2,514 in 1964.[20] Catholic congregations have, therefore, remained at ten or eleven times the size of the Protestant.

Catholic education. The vital center of American Catholicism is no longer the altar or the church: it has shifted to the school, which, from the kindergarten through the university, is designed, insofar as possible, to segregate Catholics from all other elements in the population.

Mission schools were established in what is now New Mexico as early as 1598 and by 1629 the Franciscans had a number of them in operation. There was a school in St. Augustine as early as 1606. The Jesuits established schools in California and in New Orleans early in the 18th century. The first in what was to become the thirteen original states was established in Maryland in 1641; and the first Jesuit college was established in 1677. During colonial times, the bishops fought vigorously (and in some instances successfully) to obtain public funds for their parochial schools; with the ratification of the Constitution, however, all such subsidies came to an end.[21]

By 1840, there were already two hundred parish schools in the United States; but it was during the next twenty or twenty-five years, with the enormous influx of Irish and German Catholics, that the parish school system underwent its first spectacular development. When the Civil War began, there were already more than a thousand of these in operation.[22]

At the first Provincial Council of the Catholic Church in Baltimore in 1829, it was declared "absolutely necessary that schools be established in which the young may be taught the principles of faith and morality, while being instructed in letters."[23] The first Plenary Council, 1852, also held in Baltimore, directed that a parochial school be established in every parish. The second such convention, held in the same city in 1875, declared that any church which did not already have such a school must provide one within two years; that priests who failed to accomplish this objective should be removed; that any parish which refused or failed to meet this requirement should be subjected to extreme censure; and that "All Catholic parents are bound to send their children to the parochial schools, unless either at home or in other Catholic schools they may sufficiently and evidently provide for the Christian education of their children, or unless it be lawful to send them to other schools on account of a sufficient cause, approved by the bishop, and with opportune cautions and remedies. As to what is a Catholic school, it is left to the judgment of the Ordinary to define."[24] Parents who failed to comply with this edict faced excommunication.

TABLE VIII (Appendix) indicates the numerical and relative growth of the Catholic and public educational systems in the United States during the last sixty-five years; it also reflects the phenomenal success of American Catholicism, especially during the last quarter of a century. The enormous Catholic defections which occurred down to 1920 ceased with the extension and reinforcement of the parochial educational system.

In 1890, Catholics made up only 13.25% of the population; but they have increased in constant progression so that today they constitute nearly 24%. During the same period, the number of American children from 5 to 17 in Catholic schools, increased from 3.6 to 12.05%; and the proportion of Catholic children in their own schools increased from 28.9 to 50.2%. And when we add to these the children in the public schools receiving instruction in Catholic doctrine during school hours, the proportion rises to approximately 90%! In the 1964-5 school year, the increase in total Catholic school enrollment over 1963-4 rose from 5,991,329 to 6,508,447, or about 9%.[25]

The Catholic Church, especially the Jesuit Order, established colleges and universities, as pointed out above. However, it is only of late that such denominational higher education has become a major factor on the American scene. By 1964-65, there were nearly 300 such centers of learning with an enrollment of 425,000, or 60,000 more than just one year earlier, an increase of 14%.[25] In 1946-49, the proportion of Catholic students in institutions of higher learning constituted only 3.8%; in fifteen short years, this proportion more than doubled, and the number of students so enrolled more than quadrupled.

An article published in the *National Catholic Register* states that "$3,231,073,804 represents the annual community value of Catholic elementary and secondary schools in the United States, according to figures prepared by the National Catholic Welfare Conference."[26] Multiply this by two or three and we have some idea of what it costs 8 or 10 million Catholic families in the United States to belong to their communion. This is also an indication of what it will cost the taxpayers of this country, should the government agree to support the sectarian schools of America.

CHAPTER II:

RELIGIOUS PROPERTY
IN BUFFALO, N.Y.

The social and religious complex. Buffalo was the first city selected for analysis of its privately owned, tax-exempt properties because it is typical of many large American cities; and because, when combined with others we have chosen, these should constitute a reasonable composite of the whole United States. It is one of those to which huge waves of Irish, Polish, Italian, and German Catholics came between 1845 and 1920, who have, to this day, largely determined the social and religious complex. Roman Catholics have for decades until quite recently comprised about 65% of all church communicants and nearly 45% of all the people, a proportion which, because of the Negro influx, has now fallen to 38 or 39%. In the whole diocese, however, Catholics constitute 50.89% of the population;[1] and in 1953-4, they dominated the metropolitan area with an overall ratio of 53.3% and 79.9% of the religious affiliates.[2]

Like some other northeastern and midwestern cities, Buffalo is gradually decaying at the core. Most of those who can have moved or are moving to the suburbs. Their place is being taken, in part, by Negroes, who have increased from an insignificant number in 1890[3] to more than 70,000 at the present time. What has happened is further emphasized in the declining census count, which shows a drop from 580,132 in 1950 to 532,769 in 1960. In 25 years, the white population declined by more than 100,000.

The tax-squeeze. Buffalo is experiencing a double tax-squeeze: not only is the existing corpus of real estate deteriorating with age, lack of repair, and inadequate replacement, but more and more

11

property is being removed from the tax-rolls. In 1930, taxable property was assessed at $1,065,500,000 and the exempt at $195,400,000,[4] or 18.3%. By 1963-64, as shown in TABLE IX (Appendix), the taxable had fallen to $1,036,123,658 and the exempt had risen to $458,371,012, or 44.2%—an amazing commentary on the success of pressure-group activity. This total of course included government property—federal, state, and local. Among the private-exempt, $42,787,460 was classified by the assessor as religious, of which $18,456,570 was Protestant, $22,999,990 Catholic, and $997,490 Hebrew. However, since this included only churches, parsonages, administrative properties, and a few others, and since a great many private schools, hospitals, and charitable organizations belong to churches, while others are secular or non-denominational, a complete reorganization of this data was necessary.

Privately owned, tax-exempt property. After the statistics in TABLE IX were released, the operation of the University of Buffalo, which was previously privately owned and which had a current assessment of $18,903,790, has been assumed by the state of New York. This reduced the total valuations placed on private schools and colleges from $42,817,070 to $23,903,280. Omitting the exemptions for railroads and fractions of veterans' homes, privately owned and wholly exempt real estate in Buffalo therefore totalled $108,613,240 and equalled 10.48% of the taxable, as shown in TABLE X (Appendix), of which $77,035,250, or 70.92%, was religious and $31,577,990, or 29.08%, was secular.

Among these secular holdings, charities and social services, assessed at $6,836,270, totaled far more than churches had invested in this category. There was also $17,048,430 in hospitals, which was nearly twice that of all churches combined; $6,332,580 in cemeteries, almost a total monopoly in this field; but only $1,360,710 in private schools and colleges, a field in which the churches had achieved complete pre-eminence. We might add that the secular charities and social services consisted of a Home for the Friendless, another for orphans, and one for retarded and needy children; the Goodwill Industries, an Association for the Blind, an institution for health research, a hospital service, a guidance center, and the headquarters for the Salvation Army

12

and the Red Cross. There were also singing societies, Boy Scouts, Girl Scouts, the Boys Club, the Y.W. and the Y.M.C.A.

Of the $77,035,250 of private, exempt property which was religiously owned, $122,730 was invested in cemeteries; $2,639,700 in charities and social services; and $8,932,790 in hospitals. The heaviest assessments were on denominational schools and colleges, with $22,552,570; and on churches, parsonages etc., which totaled $42,787,460.

The denominational breakdown. The statistics in TABLE X do not allocate the religious property according to denominational ownership; this, however, is done in TABLE XI (Appendix). This shows that Jewish religious property totaled $2,385,730 in assessed valuation, of which $99,490 was invested in synagogues, $811,460 in homes for the aged, $559,750 in social services (a community center, etc.); $3,910 in cemeteries and $11,120 in an educational project. The Protestant total of $19,702,920 was invested almost entirely in churches and parsonages, with only $1,246,550 for old people's homes, schools, hospitals, and cemeteries, most of which are Lutheran. The Catholic properties show an assessed valuation of $54,948,600, of which $23,333,400 was invested in churches, rectories, religious houses, and administrative agencies, which included the episcopal mansion, the diocesan headquarters at 35 Niagara Circle, a publishing enterprise, and various other items. In addition, $22,226,380 was invested in schools, seminaries, and colleges, $8,806,370 in hospitals, $22,830 in cemeteries, and $559,620 in "charities," which consisted, for the most part, of residences housing members of religious orders.

We have here an accurate reflection of the comparative denominational strength in Buffalo and the purposes for which their properties are used: the Catholics owned 71.32% of the visible religious wealth, of which some 99% was concentrated in churches, schools, hospitals, administrative agencies, and religious houses. The Jews had only 3.09% of it and all others only 25.57%.

The Catholic expansion. The Official Catholic Directory, published by the P. J. Kenedy and Sons Publishing Company of New York, and a similar forerunner by others, has appeared annually for nearly 150 years and contains a mine of information.

13

Research in this source and in the 1890 census and in the 1906 and 1936 *Census of Religious Bodies,* published by the United States Department of Commerce, has resulted in the data compiled in TABLE XII (Appendix), which reflects in detail how the Catholic Church has grown both in the city and the diocese of Buffalo, in the latter of which, between 1891 and 1964, Catholics increased from 160,000 to 897,200 and the total diocesan school enrollment from 17,435 to 108,705. This table establishes that:

(1) The proportion of Catholic students in Buffalo attending sectarian elementary and secondary schools, in comparison to the whole Catholic population, increased sharply from 9.2% in 1891 to 21.2% in 1964; and, when we add the college students, the ratio rose to 23.7%. However, outside the city, attendance, by the same measurement, declined from 20.1% in 1906 to 8.8% in 1964.

(2) Whereas in 1891 Catholic education was limited to parochial schooling, almost entirely on the elementary level, by 1964 more than one third of the enrollment was in diocesan or private high schools, or in seminaries, colleges, and universities.

(3) The ratio of Catholics in full-time sectarian schools in 1963-64 was almost three times as great in Buffalo (23.7%) as in the outlying areas (8.8%) ; and that Catholics attending public schools beyond the city limits must have outnumbered by far those in the parochial schools. Buffalo itself, with about 200,000 Catholics, had a total school enrollment of 47,408; while the 697,200 Catholics in the diocese but outside the city had a comparable total of only 61,297.

It is therefore reasonable to conclude

a. that practically all Catholic children in Buffalo attended denominational schools;

b. that almost all the 92,586 public school pupils in the diocese who received Catholic religious instruction under released time during school hours lived outside the city; and

c. that all these combined constituted very nearly all the Catholic children attending public schools; for, when we add these to the totals attending church schools, the ratio is approximately the same in the whole diocese as in the city alone.

The comparative development. TABLE XIII (Appendix) delineates the denominational growth and decline in Buffalo between 1906 and 1964; and it shows that even after the ratio as well as the actual number of Catholics declined, their properties increased in value to a fantastic degree, rising from $4,844,744, or 42.96%, to $54,948,600, or 71.32%, of the total during this period; and also that the average congregational wealth was augmented from $96,895 in 1906 to $742,549 in 1964, an increase of 755%. In contrast, the assessed value of Protestant properties, in spite of the 150% or more of inflation which has taken place, actually declined in recorded value from $26,143,258 in 1936 to $19,702,920 in 1964, a drop of 24.5% in apparent dollar value, while the corresponding Catholic totals increased from $11,746,358 to an amazing $54,948,600, or 367%. When we reduce these sums to 1936 dollars, the Protestant total becomes $7,881,168, an actual loss of 69.85%; the Catholic total becomes $21,947,440, a gain of 87.12%. In other words, according to these official records, the real Protestant wealth in Buffalo in 1964 was only slightly more than one-fourth of what it was in 1936; meanwhile, the Catholic holdings almost doubled.

The parochial and the public school. There is another very important factor which should be considered: the relationship between the public and the Catholic school system of Buffalo. The 200,000 or so Catholics who lived there in 1964 constituted approximately 38% of the population; let us see, then, what proportions of the school enrollment attended the parallel and, in effect, competing systems of education.

TABLE XIV (Appendix) indicates that:

(1) Even though the Catholic percentage in the Buffalo population has been declining since 1916, the ratio of denominational school enrollment has been increasing constantly. The ratio of public to total school attendance dropped from 78.5% in 1891 to 70.3% in 1936 and 61.4% in 1960; and the number of enrollees from 83,672 to 67,583 between 1936 and 1960. During the latter period, the comparable Catholic attendance increased from 35,514 to 42,407 and the proportion to the total from 29.5 to 38.6%, even while the Catholic ratio in the whole population was falling.

(2) We may reasonably conclude that the Catholic hierarchy has been wholly successful in Buffalo in securing parental com-

15

pliance with Church law, which forbids attendance of Catholic children at public schools (except under extreme circumstances and with the specific permission of the bishop). Since the 38% of the population which was Catholic in 1964 sent 38.6% of the entire city elementary and secondary school enrollment to their own church schools, it is certain that virtually no Catholics were enrolled in the public schools.

(3) It is very likely that the parochial schools of Buffalo were overcrowded or of inferior construction, since they showed an average assessed valuation per pupil of only $399 in 1964, compared to $758 for each enrollee in the public schools.

(4) However, since we know from TABLE XII that 92,586 Catholics in public schools were receiving sectarian instruction under released time in the diocese, we conclude that there was a dire shortage of parochial school facilities in the outlying areas; and that this was and is the apparent reason for the intense drive of the bishops to obtain public funds for their educational system.

The school vs. the church. The vital importance to the hierarchy of maintaining its schools is illustrated by what has been happening in Buffalo as more and more Catholics have moved to the suburbs. Two generations ago, the Catholic authorities were still building magnificent churches; but these are no longer the prime necessity. Just beyond the city limits, there were in 1964 new Catholic schools of superior construction, with no churches at all. In one case, a small, glass-enclosed altar, replete with candles and statues, was observed, mounted on a truck, from which Mass was administered in the open air in the yard behind a parochial school. Before the school was completed, this rite had been celebrated in a parking lot nearby.

The school, therefore, has become all-important, since Catholic children must, if possible, be segregated from the "mixed schools." Protestant children, however, rub shoulders with all others in the public schools and still retain their faith. It appears, moreover, that Protestant churches and even individual evangelists are able to make converts and obtain adherents in large numbers from the general public, a feat which has proved virtually impossible for the Catholic Church.

The minimized wealth. A few words may be pertinent concerning the magnitude of the visible Catholic wealth in Buffalo. Experts agree that this has been drastically undervalued, particularly in comparison with taxable properties. Assessments in New York state are supposed to be 49% of true or cash value. In many cases, however, valuations are far in excess of that proportion. For example, the 40-year-old Statler-Hilton Hotel, with 1100 rooms, was given an assessment of $4,926,290 or $4,478 a room, which called for an annual levy of about $335,000, more than $300 for every room. (The Supreme Court forced a reduction to $4,067,090.) The assessors, desperate for funds to operate a city with an ever-increasing percentage of exempt property, have placed the heaviest possible burdens upon those who cannot escape or who are deemed able to pay. The assessment on the Statler surpassed its original cost; it was fully 50% of current replacement value in new construction, and would allow nothing for depreciation or obsolescence; nor did the assessors consider the original cost as a basis for valuation. The older, second-rate Lafayette Hotel, with 380 rooms, was assessed at $1,151,930, or more than $3,000 per room, more than 50% of replacement value and extremely high. With a tax rate of 68 mills, an ordinary decent home in a good neighborhood pays a tax of about $1,200 a year, a crushing burden indeed.

There can be no reason for under-assessing the property of a church other than to minimize its wealth. But this can be a significant motivation among church-minded public officials; for in many countries, top-heavy church properties have eventually resulted in expropriation, accompanied by social upheavals and political revolutions.

Catholic real estate in Buffalo appeared to carry extremely low assessments. For example, just across from the Statler is the Catholic Center of the Diocese of Buffalo. This building, somewhat older than the hotel, is more than a tenth as large and should have been assessed at least in that proportion. However, the amount was only $88,950, whereas, on a comparable basis, it would have been at least $400,000. The bishop's $250,000 mansion at 25 Lincoln Parkway (exempt from local property taxes because a small altar was installed) was modestly assessed at $50,800. Canisius High School, with spacious grounds and an investment of millions, was assessed at $1,268,520; and Canisius

17

College, with an enrollment of about 3,000 and a plant worth between $20 and $30 million was assessed at $3,242,440.

The Louise de Marillac Hospital, known also as the Sisters of Mercy Hospital, was making some comparatively modest additions during 1964, which a large sign proclaimed were costing $6,500,000. The total assessment was $3,464,050. The most bizarre of the valuations observed, however, was that on St. Joseph Academy at 2064 Main Street, with about 800 students, mostly resident on the campus. It owns acres of extremely valuable land, and buildings which, altogether, bulk as large as or larger than the Statler-Hilton: *the assessment was $278,000!*

Catholic real estate in Buffalo, therefore, assessed at just under $55 million, must have a replacement value, even allowing for depreciation and obsolescence, of at least four or five times this sum. It cannot be less than $225 million; it may well be a great deal more.

CHAPTER III:

RELIGIOUS PROPERTY
IN THE DISTRICT OF
COLUMBIA

The federal complex. Washington, D.C., was selected as the second city for analysis because it reflects our whole culture and because its denominational development parallels that of many other cities. The District is a real estate anomaly because the federal government owns almost one third of all the real estate. In Buffalo, as we noted, the ratio of exempt to taxable property was 44.2%; in Washington, if we exclude the federal, the comparable proportion was 25.2%; if we include it, 83.1%.

In fiscal 1963-4, the District levied about $63 million in real estate taxes, to which the national government added a grant of $37,297,031. TABLE XV (Appendix) shows that the total assessment was $4,653,591,031, of which 54.3%, or $2,525,485,494, was on taxable property; of the 45.7% which was exempt, 32%, with an assessment of $1,491,881,236, was federal; 5%, valued at $231,518,788, belonged to the District; and 8.7%, assessed at $404,705,513, was privately owned.

The exempt properties. TABLE XV also offers a breakdown of this private property, of which 32.5%, or $131,551,270, listed as religious, includes churches, rectories, parochial schools, seminaries, religious houses, etc.; 25.3%, or $102,306,795, is educational, and includes private schools, colleges, and universities; 8.2%, or $33,198,153, is listed under foreign governments; 5.1%, or $20,531,488, is classified under the heading of charities; 12.2%, or $49,205,669, is included under hospitals; 1.8%, or $7,497,535, under cemeteries; .8%, or $3,136,075, under libraries; and 14.1% or $57,278,565, under miscellaneous.

Since this table does not show which of the properties are

19

secular and which denominational, they are so segregated in TABLE XVI (Appendix). The religious property, assessed at $221,923,408, constitutes 54.84% of the total; and the secular, valued at $182,782,105, comprises 45.16%.

Among the secular properties, such universities as George Washington and Howard and branches of Johns Hopkins and Harvard, together with smaller private schools, accounted for valuations totalling $42,643,111. Legations and embassies of foreign governments were assessed at $32,612,744. A variety of charitable enterprises were assessed at $11,735,369 and included homes for foundlings, widows, the blind, and the aged; orphanages operated by the Masons, the Oddfellows, etc.; a Florence Crittenden Home and a Home for Incurables. We had the Goodwill Industries, the Planned Parenthood Association, the Salvation Army, various missions and social settlement agencies, the Boys Club, the Visiting Nurses Association, the Thrift Shop, the Volunteers of America, and the Society for Crippled Children. All of these, which have their counterparts in most large American cities, are true charities, since they have no concern except for human welfare and make no attempt to inculcate any particular creed or doctrine.

The secular cemeteries were assessed at $3,687,426 and approximated half the property in this category. And, finally, we had, as we might expect in our national capital, a great number and variety of scientific, social, and cultural organizations whose properties are listed under miscellaneous-exempt and assessed at $57,278,565; among these, the National Geographic Society, the Brookings Institute, and the Freer and the Corcoran Gallery of Art are typical. There was also the Great Falls Museum, Anderson House, and the House Where Lincoln Died; and there were splendid facilities belonging to various fraternal orders, such as the Masons, the Oddfellows, and the L.O.O.M. The American Red Cross has its national headquarters here, and it is, of course, exempt from taxation.

The division of religious properties. This brings us to the most vital aspect of our study: the segregation of the denominational holdings, which is accomplished in TABLE XVII (Appendix). This shows that in 1964 3.31% of these were Jewish, 40.89% Protestant, and 55.79% Catholic. This Jewish portion carried an assessment of $7,367,013, of which $4,970,343 was invested in synagogues, $517,865 in schools, and $316,422 in cemeteries. The charities, assessed at $1,562,383, consisted chiefly of a Community Center and homes for the aged.

Protestant wealth. Among Protestant holdings, which totaled $90,747,315, we find hospitals, assessed at $2,134,214, owned by Seventh-Day Adventists and Episcopalians. There were cemeteries assessed at $998,153; Methodists, Presbyterians, Disciples of Christ, Episcopalians, and Lutherans owned orphanages and homes for the elderly valued at $3,691,874. There were educational properties assessed at $9,028,290, among which the Methodist American University was by far the largest, the only other of consequence being the Sidwell Friends School.

As usual, among Protestants, their overwhelming religious investments consisted of churches, of which there were 328, assessed at $74,894,784. We should note that among these the great Episcopal Washington Cathedral, assessed at $16,371,300, is a national foundation without a local congregation. It constituted 65% of all Episcopal property and 22% of all Protestant in the District. We should note also that the Catholic Shrine of the Immaculate Conception, the most magnificent church of that faith on the American continent, is also national and serves no parish. When, therefore, we use the statistics of the District as a base from which to extrapolate the value of religious property in the United States, we exclude these shrines from the computations. Subtracting them, the Protestant properties had an assessed total of $74,376,015 and the Catholic $112,779,519.

The Catholic holdings. The Apostolic Delegate of the Holy See occupies a spacious mansion at 3339 Massachusetts Avenue which was assessed at $585,409; this is exempted from taxation as property belonging to a foreign government and is the only religious item in this category. Cemeteries were assessed at $2,495,534 and two large hospitals—the Georgetown and Providence—at $15,380,643. Properties listed as charities were assessed at $3,534,822, and included the House of the Good Shepherd for wayward girls and the similar St. Joseph's Home and School for Boys, some vacant land belonging to the Marist Society, St. Vincent's Orphanage, the Convent of Bon Secours, and some residences for members of religious orders, all of which are

21

dedicated to sectarian purposes and calculated to strengthen and preserve the Church. Strangely enough, the magnificent high-rise headquarters of the National Catholic Welfare Conference, the chief directive agency of national activity, located at 1312 Massachusetts Avenue and assessed at $985,653, is accorded local tax-immunity as a charity.

Of the $51,686,143 of assessed valuation invested in churches, rectories, seminaries, convents, monasteries, and administrative agencies, we have the following breakdown: $11,029,561 for the Shrine of the Immaculate Conception; $24,677,902 in 38 parish churches, together with their rectories and 31 parochial schools; and $15,978,680 in convents, monasteries, seminaries, and related facilities. Finally, the $50,117,529 valuation placed on its educational complex represents a variety of colleges, universities, academies, and high schools. Georgetown U. and the Catholic University of America with a combined assessment of $34,882,878 head the list; Trinity, Holy Cross, Gonzaga, and Holy Redeemer are among the colleges; and Mackin, Notre Dame, St. Cecilia's, and St. John's are among the larger academies and diocesan and private high schools.

The historic development. Washington is another of those eastern cities into which large numbers of immigrants arrived from Europe during the second half of the 19th century; and the result was that by 1890, in a population of 230,392, of whom 94,203, or 40.92%, were church communicants, there were 37,502 Catholics, who comprised 16.35% of the population and 39.9% of all religious affiliates.[1] The Baptists and the Methodists were the next most numerous groups, but their combined total was considerably less than the Catholic.

TABLE XVIII (Appendix) depicts the comparative denominational development in wealth and membership which has taken place in the District since 1906. Between that year and 1964, the population increased from 307,000 to 760,000 and church communicants (who have varied between 45 and 48%) from 136,759 to about 350,500. While Jewish membership increased from 698 to about 45,000 and their congregations from 4 to 12, their proportion in the population rose from one half of one per cent to 5.8% and their ratio to all communicants from .52 to 12.8%. Protestants, who have hovered around 30% of the population and 65% of the communicants for sixty years, increased in number from 92,283 to about 225,000; they had 274 churches in 1906, 410 in 1936, but only 328 in 1964. In 1953-4, there were 60,000 Jews and 205,075 Protestants, etc., in the District (Appendix, TABLE XVIII, Note 5).

Catholic membership grew from 43,788 in 1906 to about 80,500 in 1964; but their ratio among all communicants has been dropping steadily. This was 39.9% in 1891, as we have noted; by 1906 it had declined to 32.39%, by 1936 to 29.6%, and finally by 1964 to about 23%. Their ratio to the whole population, which was 16.35% in 1890, has shown a similar decline, and fell to 14.4% in 1936. While Catholics comprised 19.5% of the population in the whole Washington archdiocese by 1964,[2] they constituted only 15.2% in the metropolitan area,[3] and less than 11% in the city itself. In 1953-4, there were 109,140 Catholics in the District;[4] but, because of the decline in total population from 802,176 in 1950 to 763,956 in 1960 and because of the white exodus to the suburbs, there cannot be more than 80,500 Catholics in the city now; and the total may be even less. Nevertheless, the number of Catholic churches increased in steady progression from 21 in 1906 to 35 in 1936 and 39 in 1964.

The economic reversal. The most challenging religious development, however, has been economic: in 1906, the Jews owned about 2.09%, the Catholics 12.55%, and the Protestants 85.36% of the religious wealth; even as late as 1936, this situation had not been radically changed, for these percentages were then 1.80, 16.62, and 81.58 respectively. Combined Protestant wealth was still five times the Catholic. The drastic alteration apparent in 1964 took place during the preceding twenty-five years. By that time, in the District of Columbia, Protestants and other groups with a combined membership exceeding 225,000, comprised almost 30% of the population and more than 64% of all church affiliates; but they owned less than 41% of the religious property; and the Catholic hierarchy, whose communicants comprised only 23% of the total and less than 11% of the population, possessed religious property assessed at $123,809,080, or 55.77% of the total. This constituted an average of $3,148,951 for each parish in the city; and represented an average congregational increase since 1906 of 5150%. In 1936, according to the government

Census of Religious Bodies, Catholics owned about 20% of the Christian religious wealth; in 1964, they owned 70% of it.

When we allow for a 150% inflation between 1936 and 1964, and reduce the latter valuations to 1936 dollars, we find that $112,777,519 in local Catholic holdings and $74,376,015 of Protestant are reduced to about $45 million and $29.7 million respectively. From the level of 1936, when there was $5,588,058 in Catholic and $27,414,495 in Protestant property, we find, therefore, an increase of $39,412,000 or 702% for the former, but of only $2,335,300 or 18.5% for all Protestants and others combined.

How representative? It is true that the District has more than its share of Catholic colleges, universities, and other properties which are national rather than local in scope. But it is also true that the 1964 ratio of Catholics in Washington was less than half of the national average; had they been proportionately as numerous in Washington as in Buffalo, Baltimore, Boston, or any one of twenty other large American cities, this one would have had, not 38 parishes, but at least sixty or seventy, each as wealthy as those which existed there. Per capita Catholic wealth in the District, therefore, was presumably little or no greater than in the country as a whole, especially since we exclude the Shrine of the Immaculate Conception from our base for computation. Even if we include only those facilities used by local Catholics, such as the churches, rectories, hospitals, cemeteries, and parochial and other lower-level schools, together with one of the universities, we have an assessed valuation in excess of $75,000,000, which makes approximately $2,000,000 for every parish.

The District schools. TABLE XIX (Appendix) compares the elementary secondary enrollment in the Catholic and public school systems. It reflects, first, the strength of this sectarian education among its own communicants, and, second, the drastic results of the Negro influx and the white exodus. In the three years following 1960, Catholic elementary enrollment dropped from 23,517 to 18,760, a loss of more than 20%. And we note that at the former date, when Catholics were already less than 13% of the population, 17.2% of the municipal enrollment was being educated in their sectarian schools. It is therefore certain that virtually no Catholic children in Washington are to be found in the public schools.

The amazing growth. It is not only the current value of Catholic property in the District which is so astonishing—even more so is its enormous expansion during recent years. The Shrine of the Immaculate Conception alone must have cost more than $30 million. Between 1961 and 1964 the valuations on all educational properties in the District zoomed from $69,823,813 to $102,306,795; and of this $33,482,892 increase, $13,935,045 was added by the two Catholic universities, of which about 65% was allocated to Georgetown U. These two institutions had a 1963-4 combined enrollment of 11,771.[5]

Assessments in the District are supposed to range from 55 to 65% of true cash or market value; and whether or not this is true of homes and commercial properties, it certainly does not hold for religiously owned real estate. All properties are theoretically reappraised every four years, but increases in assessments, caused by inflation and rising land values, have not kept pace with expanding prices. For example, the Episcopal Washington Cathedral, now 75% complete, will cost at least another $15 million; and, when done, will have a life-expectancy of 2,000 years. It was assessed in 1964 at 36% of replacement value. The Shrine of the Immaculate Conception is on the rolls at the same proportion. Furthermore, we know that the 173-year-old Georgetown U. recently completed a $21 million-improvement program;[6] yet the valuation was increased by only $8,909,000, part of which was for increased land-valuations. The total assessment is now $19,988,272 on a plant with a physical value of not less than $60 million.

Fantastic wealth. The preceding, together with much supporting data, establishes that the physical value of religiously used real estate in Washington is probably at least three times its assessment, and totaled more than $600 million in 1964, of which approximately $270 million was Protestant and $360 million Catholic.

It may also be noted that the District assessors are by no means as lenient as some of their counterparts in other cities. For example, they attempted to tax the Ethical Society for its property

25

on the ground that its members do not believe in the existence of a personal supreme being and do not, therefore, constitute a church; but the Supreme Court ruled in favor of the Society. An attempt was also made to tax the publishing house of the Catholic University of America, but the press won exemption from the same tribunal as a scientific institution. However, since each church is allowed only one exempt parsonage, Washington is dotted with Catholic rectories not listed on the exempt tax-rolls.

We cannot know the extent of religious wealth which exists in the form of stocks, bonds, cash, mortgages, etc. But we do know that an agency of the Catholic Church already owns the Potomac Plaza, a large residential project; and that the Società Generale Immobiliere, a Vatican-controlled and Italian-based international real estate development cartel, the largest of its kind in the world, is now constructing the Watergate Project near the Lincoln Memorial, on the east bank of the Potomac. This is being built on a ten-acre site and will include five huge buildings, with restaurants, a shopping center, and about 1300 luxurious apartments, to be constructed at a cost of at least $70 million, and to be sold at from $17,000 to $200,000 each.[7]

A reasonable estimate is that the replacement value of visible Catholic properties in the District of Columbia will soon be approaching the astronomical total of $500 million.

CHAPTER IV:

TAX-EXEMPT RELIGIOUS
PROPERTY IN BALTIMORE

Our third city. Roman Catholic strength in this country was first concentrated in Baltimore and its episcopate was accorded priority by the Vatican in 1858 over all other dioceses here;[1] yet its population is not predominantly of this faith. The Calvert family of English noblemen abandoned the Anglican Church for Catholicism in 1625; and its head, the second Lord Baltimore, established the colony which has grown into a great city and still bears his name.

Baltimore has long possessed a large Negro community; it comprised 67,000 in 1890 when other large northern cities still counted members of this race in the hundreds; they numbered about 167,000, or 19%, in 1936; 229,000, or 24%, in 1950; and 329,000, or 35%, in 1960.[2] Since Negroes are predominantly Protestant, there has been a large increase in the number of churches and communicants in that faith during recent years. And some might have expected a proportional reduction in Catholic and an equal increase in Protestant power, wealth, and influence; the development, however, has been the exact reverse.

Baltimore is distinguished by its great Johns Hopkins University and Hospital, which, with an assessment of nearly $30 million, accounts for more than 5% of all exempt property; and for one half of all such wealth in the privately owned secular division.

The religious complex. The visitor is impressed also by the number and size of churches and other religious properties, Jewish, Protestant, and Catholic. In 1964, there were no less than 619 individual congregations, of which 40 were Jewish, 70

27

Roman Catholic, and 509 of Protestant or miscellaneous denominations. The Jews have a number of beautiful synagogues and have provided extraordinary facilities for the care of their aged. Protestant churches are everywhere; and even though many are very modest and others quite old, some are large and in some instances very impressive. The Catholics, however, possess the bulk of the religious property, which is concentrated in churches, hospitals, and educational facilities. The magnificent, recently completed Cathedral of Mary Our Queen at 5200 N. Charles Street was assessed at $6,650,000 in 1964 and represented an investment equal to one fifth of the property belonging to 509 Protestant congregations.

Categories of exempt property. TABLE XX (Appendix) lists sixteen types of exempt property in Baltimore, which carried total valuations of $578,997,400, a ratio of 28.86% to the taxable, which was assessed at $2,006,208,768.

In this study, we are concerned only with the seven privately owned categories. TABLE XXI (Appendix) divides these, assessed at $203,679,910, according to their secular or religious ownership, of which the former totaled $59,460,620, or 29.19% and the latter $144,219,290, or 70.81%. They are classified as churches (#4), educational institutions (#5), cemeteries (#6), benevolent and cultural societies (#7), hospitals, dispensaries, and infirmaries (#8), homes and asylums (#12), and miscellaneous (#13).

Under the secular miscellaneous, assessed at $3,059,470, we have the Y.W. and Y.M.C.A., the Salvation Army, Girl and Boy Scouts, the Goodwill Industries, the Red Cross, the Baltimore League for Crippled Children, the Planned Parenthood Association, and many others. Secular homes and asylums, assessed at $1,015,980, includes the Children's Home of Baltimore, the Florence Crittenden Mission, and the American Rescue Workers.

Among secular hospitals, with a total valuation of $23,567,540, the Johns Hopkins, with an assessment of nearly $11 million in 1964, is the largest; but there were others of importance, such as the Maryland Hospital, the Children's Rehabilitation Institute, the Union Memorial, the Hospital for Women, and the South Baltimore. There was a great variety of secular lodges and benevolent and cultural associations with a combined assessment of

$5,679,920, among which fraternal orders, such as the Masons, Elks, Eagles, Oddfellows, and Moose, were prominent. The American Legion and the Norwegian Seamen had considerable property in this category; and for some reason the Peabody Institute, a liberal arts college with 360 students, was also included.

Cemeteries were divided almost equally between the religious and the non-denominational, the latter of which were assessed at $2,547,970.

Among secular colleges and universities with a total assessment of $23,589,740, Johns Hopkins is pre-eminent, with a 1964 assessment of almost $20 million.

The religious division. We see, therefore, that in spite of the great Johns Hopkins complex, nearly 71% of all privately owned, exempt property in Baltimore was religiously owned. TABLE XXII, in segregating this, shows an assessed valuation of $24,651,560, or 17.09% for Jewish property; $45,549,090, or 31.59% for Protestant; and $74,018,640, or 51.32%, for Catholic.

Each of these major divisions reflects the basic interests and purposes of its respective group. It is obvious that the Jews use the public schools and the secular hospitals, but take care of their own in other ways from the cradle to the grave. For they have $7,416,360 in synagogues, $881,860 in schools preparing professionals for the rabbinate, almost $15 million in residential retirement facilities, and $1,190,940 in cemeteries.

The Protestants had $1,010,600 in miscellaneous charities, $608,400 in homes and asylums, a mere $138,050 in cemeteries, $786,060 in denominational colleges, and $1,076,640 in various benevolences. There was a Lutheran hospital assessed at more than $3.3 million; and another, owned by the Methodists, valued at about $3.9 million. It was, however, in their churches that the Protestants concentrated their investments: these were assessed at $34,661,780.

Catholic churches, rectories, parochial schools, religious houses, and administrative agencies were assessed at $47,362,810; colleges, led by Loyola and Notre Dame, together with a number of private and diocesan and private high schools, at $7,884,950; cemeteries at $700,570; and a few benevolences at $926,510. The hospitals, with Mercy, Bon Secours, St. Agnes, and Jenkins Memorial in the lead, were assessed at $12,323,980. Miscellaneous Catholic charities were assessed at $157,420; and their homes and asylums, valued at $4,672,400, consisted of a House of the Good Shepherd, a St. Vincent's and a St. Anthony's Orphanage, the Seton Institute, and seven or eight residences housing members of religious orders.

The denominational development. TABLE XXIII (Appendix) delineates the comparative denominational development which has taken place in Baltimore. It is clear that the churches have experienced a steady growth, for the congregations increased in number from 443 in 1906 to 619 in 1964, the inclusive membership from about 270,000 to approximately 516,000, and the religious investments in real estate from $15,198,810 to $144,219,390. The ratio of church affiliates, which remained at around 50% until recently, has now risen to about 54 or 55%.

One of the distinctive elements in the religious life of Baltimore is the large influx of Jews, who increased from 75 communicants with 2 synagogues in 1906 to 73,000 with 59 houses of worship in 1936, when they constituted 8.73% of the population and nearly 17% of all communicants, a much higher ratio than in the country as a whole. By 1964, synagogues had fallen to 40, presumably because of consolidation and the movement to the suburbs; however, their denominational wealth comprised an astonishing 17.09% of the total.

In estimating the number of church communicants in 1964, we should consider the social changes which have taken place. We know that the white population declined by 75,000 and Negroes increased by 162,000 between 1936 and 1960.[3] Assuming, then, that Jews declined about 10%, that the Negro influx was 75% Protestant, and that a normal expansion of Catholics among the white population continued, we conclude that there would be, in 1964, in Baltimore, an inclusive membership of about 66,000 Jews, who made up 7.03% of the population and 12.79% of the communicants; something like 250,000 Protestants, who comprised about 27% of the population and 48.5% of the communicants; and 200,000 Catholics, who constituted approximately 21% of the population and 38% of the religious affiliates.

Protestant congregations increased in number from 400 to 509 between 1906 and 1964, while their proportionate membership, which dipped in 1936, increased by 1964 to something less than 50%. In the meantime, their wealth increased from $12,204,010 to $45,549,090.

It is interesting to note that the Catholic ratio to all church communicants dropped steadily from 45.26% in 1906 to 43.56% in 1936 and to about 38% in 1964; and their proportion in the population from 22.64 to 22.34 and finally, as we have seen, to about 21%.

It is only when we contrast the Catholic economic development with the Protestant, however, that we comprehend fully the drastic reversal which has taken place. In 1906, the Protestants owned 80.29% of the religious property; in 1936, 58.15%; and in 1964, only 31.59%! During the same period, Catholic parishes increased in number from 41 to 70; their properties from $2,984,800 to $74,018,640, or 2372%; their average wealth for each congregation from $72,800 to $1,057,409, or 1353%; their proportion of the religious wealth from 19.64% in 1906 to 30.8% in 1936 and 51.32% in 1964. In the same period, Protestant wealth increased from $12,204,010 to $45,549,090, or 273%, and that of the average congregation from $30,510 to $89,487, or 193%; however, whereas in 1906 they owned more than 80% of the combined Catholic-Protestant wealth, in 1964 their share of this had shrunk to 38% of the assessed valuation.

The spectacular development which has taken place is even more strongly emphasized when we compute the 150% inflation which has occurred. TABLE XXIV reduces 1964 values to 1936 dollars; and, by so doing, shows that the 1964 value of Jewish religious property in Baltimore, in terms of 1936 dollars, was $9,860,664, which constituted a gain of 173.9% over the $3.6 million of 1936; the Catholic becomes $29,607,456, which was a 195.1% advance over the $10,032,052 of the earlier date; but the Protestant wealth is actually reduced to $18,219,636, which is a loss of $719,372, or 3.8% from the 1936 level. And so the total religious wealth of an estimated 250,000 Protestants living in Baltimore in 1964 is less than that of the 172,313 who resided there in 1936. And while their per capita investment, in terms of 1936 dollars, dropped from $110 to $73 during this 28-year period, that of Catholics increased from $53 to $148. In terms of current dollars, per capita Protestant investment increased from $82 in 1906 to $182 in 1964; Jewish from $133 to $374; and

31

Catholic from $24 to $370. Nothing could place in sharper relief the comparative development which has occurred in the principal denominations.

The educational complex. TABLE XXV (Appendix) presents statistics which reflect the growth of the Catholic educational system. By 1964, this had become so large in the city and the diocese of Baltimore and extended so far into the upper echelons of learning that it constituted an entire, competing complex. In addition to 56 church-attached (parochial) schools with a total of 30,967 pupils, almost all on the elementary level, there were eleven private or diocesan high schools, with an enrollment of 8,508; among these, the Archbishop Curley High School with 817 students, the Calvert School with 1250, the Catholic High School with 1124, the Mercy High with 1050, Mt. St. Joseph's Academy with 1180, and Seton High with 1113 were typical. Among seminaries and colleges, which had a combined enrollment of 4,375, Loyola, distinguished by its magnificent church, had 2310 students; St. Mary's had 612; the College of Notre Dame, 962; and Mt. St. Agnes College, 438.[4]

We find, therefore, that in Baltimore, with a 1964 population of 939,000, there were some 200,000 Catholics, of whom 39,475, or 19.74%, were students enrolled in their own elementary and secondary schools; and that a total of 43,850, or almost 22%, were undergoing full-time instruction in denominational schools. We find, further, that Catholics, who comprised about 21% of the population, had 18.4% of the entire elementary and secondary school enrollment of the city in their sectarian schools, and this in spite of the fact that some 330,000 Negroes had a double ratio of school-age children.[5] And we find that the proportion of Catholics in school (21.93%) was very nearly the same as for the entire population (22.9%).

TABLE XXV shows also that of the 429,375 Catholics in the diocese, 82,685, or 19.3%, were enrolled in full-time denominational schools at some level; that 17,253 public school students (all probably outside Baltimore) were receiving religious instruction during school hours under released time; that a total of 99,938, or 23.3% of all Catholics, were undergoing sectarian instruction; and that 83% of these were in full-time Catholic schools.

These statistics reveal, in addition, that in 1906 12.8% of all Catholics in Baltimore were in full-time, denominational schools, a proportion which increased to almost 20% by 1964; and that in the whole diocese the proportion rose from 10.5% to 19.3%, which indicates an almost full development of this educational system throughout. We note, finally, that in advanced education, the ratio in Catholic schools was even higher; for, while 18.4% of all the elementary and secondary pupils were in Catholic schools, 20.59% of all advanced students in the city were in Catholic colleges. Six secular institutions of higher learning in Baltimore, with Johns Hopkins and the University of Baltimore at the front, had 16,862 students,[6] while Catholic colleges had 4,375.

We should note also that after 1936 the archdiocese of Baltimore was divided by the creation of the Washington jurisdiction. The result was that 172 parishes with 138 parochial schools were reduced to 126 and 107 respectively; however, the number of Catholics in the smaller area remaining to Baltimore increased from 349,226 in 1936 to 429,403 in 1964 and the number of students under full-time Catholic instruction from 66,603 to 82,685.

The denominational real estate in Baltimore. Since the assessed valuation of exempt property in Baltimore does not exceed 45 or 50% of the true, cash, or market value, even while making due allowance for depreciation and obsolescence, the 1964 physical value of exempt religious property must total about $300 million, of which the Jewish portion was about $50 million, the Protestant $90 million, and the Catholic $150 million. The true value may have been considerably higher; and this means that the average Catholic wealth in Baltimore for each parish was well in excess of $2 million. Even so, the most significant factor is the ascent of the Catholic hierarchy from real as well as comparative poverty as late as 1906 and even 1936 to its 1964 position of overwhelming affluence. This fact is the more extraordinary because of the minority status of the Catholics in Baltimore; and because both the Protestants and the secularists constitute a seemingly vigorous and prosperous majority, who occupy a far stronger position than in most of the great American metropolises.

CHAPTER V:

TAX-EXEMPT RELIGIOUS
PROPERTY IN DENVER

An epitome of American culture. For balance in this study, the analysis of one western city was imperative; and Denver was selected, partly because it shows no deterioration at the center. It is scarcely affected by a recent slight influx of Negroes, since it has had an established community of these for many years and since even now they constitute only about 7% of the population. Furthermore, this city is highly representative of the American development in general, because, in its constant growth, it has absorbed the basic characteristics of her culture. Finally, it stands out in sharp relief against such places as Buffalo, which many years ago became heavily Catholic: for the "Capital of the Rocky Mountain Empire" was settled and organized by Protestants, who have always been socially, economically, and politically predominant.

The phenomenal expansion into pre-eminence of Catholic power, influence, and comparative wealth which has occurred in many portions of the United States has not been consummated in this city, where the situation is still very similar to what existed elsewhere between 1926 and 1936. In Denver, therefore, we can view in miniature the American religious complex very nearly as it was forty years ago.

The city and county of Denver are identical, had 493,837 inhabitants in 1960, and are surrounded by suburbs which have a population of some 300,000. In this study, however, we deal with the city only, which had 395 churches in 1964, of which 38 were Catholic, 10 Jewish and 347 Protestant or miscellaneous.

The suburbs had 328 churches, of which only 12 were Catholic.
The Protestant priority. In Denver, the Jews were late arrivals, but their recent expansion has been astonishing. After modest beginnings, the Catholics have now also achieved greatly increased importance. In the early days, however, it was the Protestants who did the building and who exercised the power. For example, the same Mr. Evans who founded Northwestern University and for whom Evanston is named arrived about 1858 and obtained a special territorial grant from the federal government; he set up an entity still known as the Colorado Seminary, which owns the University of Denver and a great many other parcels of tax-free property, many of them commercial. The assessed valuation of these totaled $8,347,170 in 1962, but grew to $12,426,260 in 1964. Although this was a Methodist project at its inception, the University is now entirely secular. The Iliff Theological Seminary, now assessed at $474,080, had the same origin as the University, but is now a separate entity, still considered Methodist-related. However, it has become so interdenominational that it is classified by the assessor as a private school, as is the Baptist-related Colorado Woman's College, assessed at $2,191,360. The elderly widow Iliff, scion of a large fortune, makes generous gifts to the Colorado Seminary from time to time. The Clayton Estate or Trust with properties assessed at $1,498,030 in 1964 is another agency which fosters education.

The exempt properties. TABLE XXVI (Appendix) reproduces the categories of exempt properties listed by the assessor's office; these totaled $215,930,660, or 18.45% of the 1962-63 taxable, which were valued at $1,169,942,550. According to the official classification, churches were assessed at $19,609,310; parochial schools at $8,479,070; hospitals at $11,519,350; fraternal organizations at $2,489,170; parsonages at $1,252,130; private schools at $3,519,770; and other charitable organizations at $7,799,100.

A reclassification. These statistics, however, issued January 1, 1963, are actually the 1962 valuations; it was, therefore, necessary, in order to obtain a correct current analysis, to transcribe all exempt assessments directly from the latest tax-rolls. This resulted in a reduced total for taxable but a large increase for exempt properties over the $64,672,120 shown in 1962.

35

TABLE XXVII (Appendix), which combines a number of categories, reproduces the assessments as they appeared on the rolls late in 1964, when the privately owned, exempt properties were assessed at $77,882,470. Among these, the Colorado Seminary and the Clayton Estate had a combined assessment of $13,924,230; churches, parsonages, religious houses, administrative agencies, and parochial schools were valued at $31,177,880; hospitals, sanatoria, etc., at $16,302,080; private schools at $3,412,700; and fraternal, charitable, and other non-profit organizations at $13,065,580. We note that while the proportion of exempt property was less than in most eastern states, the same process is going on in Denver which has become a common phenomenon throughout the nation; while the assessments on taxable properties fell by $17,574,080, the valuations on the privately owned and exempt increased by $13,210,350, or 20.42%, in less than 2 years. The result is that Denver, like many other communities, is experiencing a serious tax-squeeze.

The division of exempt properties. TABLE XXVIII (Appendix) segregates the exempt secular at $25,164,730, or 32.31%, and the religious at $52,717,740, or 67.69%—proportions which approximate those in Buffalo and Baltimore.

The secular schools, colleges, and universities, assessed at $14,681,490, consist largely of the holdings of the Colorado Seminary and the Clayton Estate. Children's Hospital was the most important of the secular facilities in this category, which had a total assessment of $3,577,840. Charitable and other non-profit properties, assessed at $6,905,400, included those of many fraternal orders, such as the Masons, Elks, Eagles, Oddfellows, etc.; the Y.M. and Y.W.C.A.; the American Legion, the Veterans of Foreign Wars, the Chamber of Commerce, the Goodwill Industries, the Red Cross, and various health services, such as the American Cancer Society, the Florence Crittenden Home, the Planned Parenthood, Alcoholics Anonymous, and the Mile-High United Fund. We have also the Denver Art Museum, the Fairmount Cemetery (secular), and the Bonfils Foundation for the Performing Arts, a beautiful facility assessed at about a half million dollars.

Exempt investment property. An unusual situation existed in Denver, for not only were the Colorado Seminary and the

36

Clayton Estate permitted to own tax-exempt commercial property: this privilege was extended also to various other organizations, both secular and religious, which operated income-producing projects, which paid neither federal nor local ad valorem property taxes. On August 16, 1964, St. John's Lutheran Church dedicated a magnificent "non-profit" apartment building at 330 Acoma St., financed by an F.H.A. loan.[1] There were already in operation seven other similar investments with a combined assessment of $2,357,500 and owned by various Protestant churches. In addition, there were five other such projects, assessed at $1,902,720, owned by unions or simply by groups who have organized for the purpose of owning and operating facilities of this nature. At the present time, there is no reason why some church or other non-profit organization could not own huge shopping centers and many other kinds of commercial property, wholly free from all local ad valorem taxes. Actually, there are already commercial "charities" with assessed valuations totalling almost $4.3 million and with a probable replacement value somewhere between $15 and 20 million.

The division of religious property. Of the $52,717,740 in assessed valuations placed on denominational property, $6,921,270, or 13.12%, was Jewish, of which $1,150,770 was invested in synagogues and denominational schools; $364,960 in other educational facilities; $4,918,960 in hospitals, for which the city long has been justly famous; $486,580 in "charities," almost all of which consisted of a Community Center and some other similar projects.

Of the $25,384,210 of Protestant wealth, which was 48.16% of the total, $3,202,960 was invested in schools, principally the Iliff Seminary, and the Colorado Woman's College, which should perhaps have been placed in the secular category. However, there were Protestant hospitals, of which the Episcopalian St. Luke's, the Adventist Porter Sanatorium, and the magnificent Presbyterian accounted for almost all of the $3,910,270 assessed upon properties in this category. Some old people's homes accounted for $273,470; and, as we have seen, apartment buildings assessed at $2,357,500 were owned by various denominations. However, as usual, the huge Protestant investment was in churches, which totaled $15,640,010, but included a few Lutheran,

37

Christian, and Seventh-Day Adventist parochial schools.

The $20,412,260 Catholic investment, which constituted 38.72% of the religious wealth, comprised, first, churches, rectories, parochial schools, convents, and administrative properties, totaling $8,364,590 in assessed valuation. We might add that this included also the properties of the *Catholic Register* at 908 Bannock Street, and the enormous mansion of Archbishop Urban J. Vehr, located at 777 Pearl Street. Under denominational schools, assessed at $5,247,520, we had Regis College, the wealthy St. Thomas Seminary, and the luxurious Loretto Heights College, with a combined enrollment of 2,156; and a number of high schools, such as Marycrest, Regis, and Mullen. The Catholics operated the huge St. Anthony's Hospital, as well as St. Joseph's and Mercy, with a total assessment of $5,098,990. The Catholic charities and asylums, valued at $1,701,160, consisted here, as elsewhere, mostly of the House of the Good Shepherd, a St. Vincent's Home for Boys, and a number of residences for members of religious orders.

The historic evolution. TABLE XXIX (Appendix) delineates the comparative denominational development which has taken place in Denver. The churches have increased in number from 175 in 1906 to 395 in 1964, and their wealth from $3,610,050 to $52,717,740. The communicants, who comprised 46.3% of the population in 1906 and 1936, increased slightly to 47.9% in 1953,[2] and an estimated 50% in 1964. The Jews increased in number from 703 in 1906, to 17,000, or 3.4% of the population, in 1964; and their religious wealth from $124,300 to an assessment of $6,921,270. Catholic communicants increased from 31,192 in 1936 to 76,612 in 1953-4,[2] and an estimated 90,000 in 1964. And even though they declined from more than 20% of the population and 44% of the communicants in 1906 (levels reached because of the large influx of Mexicans) to 13.4 and 28.9% respectively by 1936, this trend has since been reversed, together with the strengthening of the parochial schools. As a result, the proportion of Catholics by 1964 had risen to 18.2% of the population and 36.4% of the religious affiliates. Although the Protestants increased slightly from 54.6 to 56.8% of all communicants and from 25.2 to 28.4% of the population between 1906 and 1964, the Catholic Church has been able to expand and consolidate its actual and relative position to an astonishing degree during these decades. In 1906, it owned only 14.34% of all religious property compared to Protestant holdings of 82.22%; in 1964, the Catholic percentage had increased to 38.72; and the Protestant had fallen to 48.14, or less than half of the total. This development took place during a period of apparent virility among Protestants and while their number increased from 38,400 to about 140,000. Yet the average wealth of their congregations, even in terms of current dollars, including schools and hospitals, increased only from $19,528 to $73,239, or 256%; while that of the average Catholic congregation increased from $39,809 to $537,164, or 1276%. In terms of 1964 values, therefore, allowing for the inflation since 1906, the individual Protestant churches have barely maintained their *status quo*. While Protestant wealth was increasing from $2,968,225 to $25,384,210, or 755%, the Catholic was growing from $517,525 to $20,412,260, or 3856%. It is evident that if this process continues, the Catholic parishes will soon possess far more wealth in Denver than is owned by all the Protestant congregations there. Since Denver assessments are only 30% of real value, the true average wealth of Jewish congregations was $2,285,000 in 1964; of Protestant churches, $242,000; and of Catholic parishes, $1,708,000. Since eight or ten of the last served poor congregations of Mexican descent, the true wealth of the others must have averaged well in excess of $2 million.

Catholic education. TABLE XXX (Appendix) shows the growth of Catholic education in Denver; but it also reflects the extraordinary effort expended by the hierarchy to educate all its youth in its own schools. In such cities as Washington, Buffalo, and Baltimore, this problem had been solved by 1964; but in Denver, and especially in its environs, this objective had not yet been attained, since the proportion of youth in the Catholic schools of the city was only 15.7% compared to a Catholic percentage in the population of 18.2. However, this gap was narrowing rapidly; for the ratio of Catholic to public school enrollment rose from 11.2% to 15.7% between 1936 and 1964; and new Catholic schools were under construction all over the city at the latter date. In the outlying portions of the diocese, however, the situation was quite different; for in the 69 parishes there, only 20% of all Catholic children were in sectarian schools. The proportion of Catholics in the whole diocese (17.8%) was almost identical to that in the city; but the 151,000 Catholics who resided beyond its limits had only about 12,000 pupils in denominational schools. The result was that in the whole diocese there were 39,311 public school pupils receiving Catholic instruction under released time and they comprised far more than half of the Catholic youth in the entire jurisdiction. And this, as we have noted, was and remains the situation which impels the hierarchy with such fervor to seek public subsidies for their schools. Most Catholic authorities consider the released-time arrangement no more than a temporary expedient at best; for this is the situation which results in a large percentage of "mixed marriages"; and these, as is very well known, often eventuate in defection from the faith.

The priority of the school. It should be noted in Denver, as in other cities and in many suburban areas, that the supreme Catholic emphasis is now on the school. No longer is it possible to retain the youth by building huge cathedrals, to which are attached inferior facilities dedicated to sectarian indoctrination. In one Catholic parish after another in Denver and its suburbs, therefore, we find literally no church at all: instead, there is a large and modern educational plant (almost on par with the public schools), of which a combination gymnasium and social hall is a part, where Mass may be celebrated and bingo played in simple surroundings. This was the case in 1964 in the parish of Notre Dame at 2707 S. Zenobia St.; the Presentation of Our Lady at 632 Julian; St. Mary Magdalene at 28th and Zenobia; Most Precious Blood at 2227 S. Colorado, and several others. The better the neighborhood, the more obvious was this development. In the poorer areas, especially among those of Mexican descent, the church and the rectory were still several times the size of the school and incomparably more costly. For example, a huge new church was under construction in the parish of St. Rose of Lima at 1320 W. Nevada; there was a small parochial school for Mexicans behind it, serving 355 pupils. Just two blocks away was the magnificent Valverde School, which these children could have attended without cost. St. Patricks Church and rectory, at 3325 Pecos Street, filled almost a whole block;

its school, however, at 3220 Pecos, which served 320 Mexican pupils, was nothing more than a converted house. It was obvious, however, by the number of Protestant churches in these Mexican areas, that many of these people must have abandoned the Catholic faith.

On the other hand, the Church of the Blessed Sacrament, at 4930 Montview, in one of Denver's finest residential neighborhoods, had just completed an excellent, modern grade school and a new high school facility, comparable to those operated by the city. And St. James at 1205 O'Neida Street had abandoned its tiny old chapel and built a magnificent new school, at which no church at all was in evidence.

A showcase for youg women. The College of Loretto Heights for girls is the Catholic showpiece of Denver. It boasts at least half a dozen impressive buildings, including a Bonfils Theater for the Performing Arts, almost a duplicate of another given by the same donor and bearing a similar name downtown. This institution has luxurious dormitories, spacious grounds, a large swimming pool, and superior class-room buildings. If there is a church or chapel on the campus, it is certainly not in sight.

The religious wealth of Denver. Since Denver assessments are about 30% of true value, exempt property in 1964 was therefore worth approximately $700 million, of which about $22 million was Jewish, $80 million Protestant, and something like $65 million under the control of the Vatican.

CHAPTER VI:

AN ESTIMATE OF TOTAL RELIGIOUS PROPERTY IN THE UNITED STATES

The changing image. This study is based on research conducted in the summer and fall of 1964; but, since religious property is expanding with kaleidoscopic speed, further drastic alterations will no doubt have occurred in three or four years. Between 1961 and 1964 in the District of Columbia, the assessments on churches increased from $113,274,614 to $131,551,270; and the valuations on two Catholic universities alone by more than $13 million. In Denver, as we have noted, the assessments on exempt properties increased by more than 20% in two years.

Protestant and Catholic properties. We have noted also that a large proportion of Catholic religious property consists of real estate other than churches and rectories; and it should be pointed out that Protestants also have had large investments in property other than church edifices and parsonages. They have owned many, and still own a few, denominational colleges; and they own a great many cemeteries, old people's homes, hospitals, publishing enterprises, etc. Two or three generations ago these would have come nearer to the value of their Catholic counterparts than they do today.

Literally hundreds of colleges and universities were founded by churches, Protestant *and* Catholic: and in the beginning, all of these could qualify as truly religious property. Countless small colleges were Protestant-oriented, as were such great universities as Harvard, Chicago, Northwestern, Purdue, U.S.C., S.M.U.,

Princeton, etc.; and in the beginning, they inculcated the doctrines of their own denominations. The significant fact is that every Catholic college and university was from its inception owned by the church itself and controlled and directed by its priesthood; each and every one of these, therefore, remains to this day an instrument of the hierarchy. The Protestant institutions, on the contrary, were organized as independent entities or non-profit corporations, controlled by their own governing boards. So long as these consisted of churchmen dependent on their denominations for their livelihood, the colleges and universities themselves remained religious institutions; but when the lay alumni assumed control and operation and when funds began to come from permanent endowments and other sources, these seats of learning were secularized. The result is that all Catholic institutions have remained strictly sectarian, but very nearly all Protestant-originated colleges and universities have become non-religious. A classic example of this development is the Colorado Seminary, which owns the University of Denver; both were once religious, but are now secular. One result is that the Catholic Church has accumulated billions in educational property; but the Protestant churches have lost an even greater potential.

Obtaining accurate results. Buffalo, Washington, Baltimore, and Denver were chosen for analysis because when taken as a single entity we believe that they represent a cross-section of religious communicants and church wealth in the United States and, therefore, constitute a reliable base for extrapolation, a method now recognized as scientific. It is not necessary to poll every voter to discover how an election will turn out; it is important, however, that the sampling be representative. For example, in 1957, the United States Bureau of the Census asked 35,000 individuals, "What is your religion?"[1] The results were in very close agreement with totals supplied by the various churches themselves.

The pilot cities. TABLE XXXI (Appendix), which, like that following, combines the statistics of the four cities, shows that they increased in population from 1,254,033 in 1906 to 2,722,000 in 1963-64, a ratio of growth almost identical to that in the nation, which increased concurrently from 85,400,000 to about 186,000,000. In the meantime, the religious communicants in-

43

creased from 671,840 to approximately 1,453,500 in the four cities, thus maintaining a constant ratio of about 54%; meanwhile, national communicants increased from 32,936,445 to 117,946,000, an increase in ratio from 38.57 to 63.41% of the population. Nationally, Protestants, etc., increased from 20,755,-846 to 68,589,065; but their ratio among all communicants dropped from 63.02 to 58.17%, a loss due, first, to an influx of Jews, who advanced from almost nothing to an official count of 5,509,000, and, second, to a vast growth in Catholic strength, which increased from 12,079,142 to 43,847,937 communicants and from a ratio of 36.67 to 37.16% among all religious affiliates. By 1964, the national Protestant-Catholic proportions had become almost exactly 60-40%; in our four cities, they were 57-43%.

According to the government census (cf. TABLE XXXII, Appendix), the religious wealth in the four cities was $40,110,946 in 1906, of which $527,300, or 1.31%, was Jewish; $29,977,027, or 74.74%, was Protestant; and $9,606,619, or 23.95%, was Catholic. By 1964, the total assessed value had risen to $468,494,827, of which $41,323,573, or 8.82%, was Jewish; $165,012,235, or 35.22%, was Protestant; and $262,159,019, or 55.96%, was Catholic. Of the combined Christian wealth, 61.4% was Catholic and 38.6% belonged to Protestant and miscellaneous denominations.

TABLES XXXI and XXXII show that the comparative religious strength in our pilot cities has, in the past, closely paralleled the national; and presumably does so still in regard to the Catholic-Protestant complex. TABLE XXXII presents a composite analysis of all religous properties together with their valuations in the four cities; and, since these have 1.46% of the national population, they are sufficient in extent to present an adequate miniature of the nation.

It is true that the individual congregations are today larger in our four cities (one for every 868 communicants) than in the country as a whole (where we have one for every 370); but, since churches are proportionately more numerous and communicants comprise a higher ratio in the population nationally (63.41%) than in our cities (53.39%), it seems reasonable to conclude that per capita religious investment is approximately equal in all areas. In 1936, in our four cities, 198 Catholic parishes constituting 1.8% of the total, owned 3.32% of their national property, and operated parish plants with an average valuation of $149,456. For the whole country, the average was $70,080. A similar pattern held true for Protestants, whose congregations in the four cities had an average wealth of $62,499 in 1936, while in the whole United States it was only $15,487. However, our cities, which had 1.73% of the total population in that year, had only .78% of the congregations; which implies that per capita religious investments outside our cities would even then have been well over half of what it was within them.

The per capita church wealth credited to communicants shows a most significant comparison and development. Nationally, such Protestant shares grew from $45 to $163 between 1906 and 1964; but for Catholics the increase was from $24 to $400. In the four cities, per capita Protestant wealth was $86 in 1906; $148 in 1936; and $224 in 1964; while for Catholics the comparable amounts were $30, $53, and $460 respectively. Thus, while per capita Protestant wealth was almost triple the Catholic nationally and almost double in the four cities in 1906 and 1936, it dropped to less than half in 1964. These statistics indicate also that an extrapolation of national Catholic-Protestant wealth on the basis of that in the four cities will be approximately accurate: and this is true because the ratio of church communicants nationally exceeds that in the four cities by approximately the same proportion as the per capita wealth of communicants there exceeds the national.

The divergent growth. TABLE XXXI shows further that the ratio of Catholic communicants in the American population increased from 14.14 to 23.57% between 1906 and 1964 and that of Protestants from 24.3 to 36.88%. This shows that while both groups grew substantially, the Catholics did so more rapidly. In our cities, however, we find a somewhat different pattern; for, although their ratio of the national population dropped from only 1.73 in 1936 to 1.46 in 1964, the number of congregations in the whole country increased after 1936 by almost 120,000, or 60%, and the number of communicants from 55,800,000 to almost 118,000,000, or 113%; meanwhile, the churches in these cities increased by only 117 or 7.5% and the communicants from 1,227,785 to about 1,453,500, or 18%. Even more significant is

45

the fact that whereas 2.22% of all communicants were in our cities in 1936, only 1.23% were there in 1964, and of these a very large number were Negroes. The ratio of Protestants there compared to the national were reduced from 1.72% in 1936 to 1.07% in 1964; and that of Catholics from 2.81% to 1.3% during the same period. Since about 3% of the national religious wealth was concentrated in the four cities by 1936, these statistics imply that no more than 1.5% could have been there in 1964. In short, per capita religious wealth in the four cities would be approximately equal to that on the national level.

The balanced wealth. We note, furthermore, that whereas Catholics made up 23.57% of the national population in 1963-4, they comprised only 20.24% in our four cities. TABLE XXXIII (Appendix) shows that 1.95% of all Catholic elementary and secondary pupils were in full-time sectarian schools in our four cities, which would indicate that these had more than their share of these; but, by the same token, their share of parishes (1.3%) was less than the national and their proportion of the 6,000 church chapels and missions was much smaller still. This would counterbalance the additional educational facilities in the four cities.

The method of extrapolation. Further examination of TABLE XXXII tends to confirm this conclusion. The proportionate Protestant-Catholic wealth in the past has been almost identical in the whole nation and in our four cities, which therefore emerge as an apparent epitome of the whole. That proportion was 74.91 to 23.25% for the whole country and 74.74 to 23.95% for our cities in 1906. In 1936, the ratio was 72.98 to 23.73% nationally and 69.00 to 25.76 in our pilot cities. It is, therefore, reasonable to conclude that whatever ratio exists between these principal religious groups in 1964 in our cities is also approximately correct for the nation. Since, therefore, the population of the four cities comprises 1.46% of the national, we simply multiply their religious wealth by 68 to obtain the approximate total for the United States.

TOTAL VISIBLE NATIONAL RELIGIOUS WEALTH

Denomination	Approximate As-sessed Valuation	% of All	Approximate True or Cash Value
Jewish	$2,800,000,000	8.80	$7,000,000,000
Protestant	11,200,000,000	35.22	28,000,000,000
Catholic	17,800,000,000	55.97	44,500,000,000
TOTAL	$31,800,000,000	100.00	$79,500,000,000

The true values. In order to find the true cash or replacement value of the religious properties, we have assumed that assessments average 40% of actual values. In Buffalo, we found that some assessments on religious real estate did not exceed 10%; in Washington, they were supposed to be about 55%, but were usually substantially less; in Baltimore, the average was about 45% and in Denver 30%. When, therefore, we multiply the combined assessments by 2.5, the result is more likely to be an under- than an overestimation. In this, of course, we do not seek exact totals, but only approximations. On this basis, Jewish religious property totals $7 billion, or an average of about $1,715,000 for each of the 4,079 congregations; Protestant churches, about $28 billion, or about $96,000 for each of the 289,899; and the Catholic about $44.5 billion, an average of approximately $2,500,000 for each of 17,445 parishes. This does not mean, of course, that each congregation, church, or parish had property with such a value at its service or disposal; it signifies simply that this is the average share for each within its denomination, and includes all schools, hospitals, cemeteries, and other religiously used real estate.

The religious division. This seems to be a fairly accurate division among the principal groups of church-owned real estate used specifically for religious purposes. It takes no account, of course, of any property on which taxes are levied; and, as we have seen, there is a great deal which falls into this category.

Since the bulk of the property belonging to Protestant denominations consists of parsonages and church edifices, the problem of estimating total wealth in this division is quite a different matter from evaluating the Catholic. TABLE XXXII indicates that the Protestant congregations had an estimated average assessed wealth in 1964 of about $38,600 (or $96,000 in

47

replacement value), which, since it covers land, auditorium, Sunday School and other facilities, seems a very modest sum indeed. And yet this is an extrapolation of properties owned largely by flourishing churches and can, therefore, scarcely be an underestimation. This is further emphasized by the fact that in 1936 the average Protestant church property in the four cities was four times as great as the average in the nation, while in the Catholic denomination the ratio was a little more than double.

Catholic wealth. Nor can our computation of national Catholic wealth be a substantial underestimate. The truth is that this denomination is rather poor in portions of our four cities compared to the wealth it possesses in such centers as Boston, Chicago, San Francisco, and New York. The last archdiocese, which consists of the boroughs of Manhattan, Bronx, and Richmond, and some territory across the Hudson in New Jersey, had, according to the 1964 *Official Catholic Directory,* a population of 4,980,000, of whom 1,782,630, or 35.8%, were Catholics, served by 402 parish churches, 602 chapels, and 15 hospitals; by 16 colleges and universities, with 23,411 students; by 99 diocesan, private, and parochial high schools, with 47,660 students, and by 322 elementary schools with 171,290 pupils. There were, of course, a great many convents, monasteries, retreats, orphanages, protective institutions, etc. In addition, 111,587 public school pupils received Catholic indoctrination under released time.[2] Nearly 355,000 students, therefore, comprising 20% of all claimed Catholics in the diocese, were under sectarian instruction.

The Protestant church and the Catholic parish. The average Protestant congregation in 1964 had 226 members, housed in a modest structure capable of accommodating about 250 in its auditorium and equipped with some accommodations for the Sunday school. At 1964 prices, the average value of such a facility, as we have seen, was about $96,000, including the land and its share in any hospital, cemetery, school, charity, etc., owned by the denomination. The standard Catholic parish, by contrast, had more than 2,500 communicants, a magnificent church, at least one impressive rectory, a convent housing its teaching sisters, and a parochial school with a capacity of some six hundred pupils. Let us say that the cost of the educational facility was $2,000 per pupil, that the value of the convent resi-

48

dence was $150,000, and the replacement cost of the church $350,000, and of the rectory $100,000; there was, then, a minimum investment of $1.8 million. Some of the larger and newer complexes involved expenditures of three, or five, or even ten million dollars. On this minimum basis, those parishes which were equipped with schools alone had wealth totalling some $20 billion. This, of course, did not include colleges, universities, hospitals, publishing enterprises, and a host of other investments. Nor did it cover the property of 9,000 altars, chapels, and missions, nor of nearly seven thousand additional parishes which had no attached educational plants.

Further computation. Let us attempt a variant method. There were about 300 Catholic colleges and universities in 1964 with an enrollment of 425,000. A $6,000 investment for each student totals $2.55 billion for higher education. An average of $2,000 for each elementary and secondary enrollee involves an investment of about $12 billion in this project. An average minimum investment of $8 million for each hospital means at least $6.5 billion in 803 of these institutions. Assuming that the average value of 17,445 parish churches and 6,000 church chapels and missions was $300,000, we have another item of nearly $7 billion. This seems a low estimate, since there are many Catholic churches in the multi-million-dollar class. For example, St. Patrick's in New York stands on land worth at least $20 million; and the building itself could not be replaced for less than $25 million. The cost of 20,000 rectories at $100,000 each adds another $2 billion. These items total at least $30 billion.

In addition, of course, the Vatican, in the names of its bishops and religious orders, possesses vast properties in the form of business enterprises or administrative agencies, and Franciscan, Dominican, Benedictine, and many other monasteries and retreats, occupied by brothers and priests; in 1964, they had residences housing almost 200,000 sisters; there are orphanages, correctional institutions, and homes for retired religious; a great chain of seminaries in which some 50,000 young men were studying for the priesthood; hundreds of cemeteries, often on very valuable land; publishing houses, diocesan headquarters, and propaganda agencies of almost infinite variety. These total many billions of additional exempt property, and, when added to that summarized in the preceding paragraph, would certainly make up something like a value of $45 billion.

The Catholic Strength. As shown in TABLE VIII, among some 45,000,000 claimed Catholics in the United States, there should have been about 11,500,000 between 5 and 17 years of age. It is therefore obvious that the hierarchy is losing very few of its people, since there were 6,000,000 pupils in full-time Catholic schools in 1964 and since about 4,500,000 others of this age who attended public schools were receiving sectarian instruction during school hours under released time. It is therefore apparent that at least 90% of all Catholic youth in the United States were undergoing intensive indoctrination in the faith.

We should emphasize that Catholic and Protestant membership are quite different: for the former is a total commitment, while the latter is only partial. In a society where the Catholic Church rules as a theocracy, there is little distinction between civil and ecclesiastical authority; and to a lesser degree everywhere members of that church are controlled and organized in every aspect of their lives under its direction. Members of Protestant churches can join by signing a card and can leave without retaliation whenever they wish; but no one can become a Catholic except by being born and reared in the church or by placing himself wholly under its indoctrination and authority. Even a minority Catholic Church is therefore in a sense a state within a state; and when it assumes majority status, it becomes actually an integral part of the state itself, and all must obey its directives or suffer serious, and sometimes the most extreme, penalties.

Summation. According to the computations here set forth, then, the current value of religiously owned Jewish wealth in the United States is about $7 billion; of Protestant, etc., $28 billion; and of Catholic, about $44.5 billion. As late as 1936, according to the official reports in the government census, Protestant wealth was still at least double the Catholic; but this study shows that by 1964 Catholic religious holdings were almost 60% greater than that of all Protestant and miscellaneous churches combined.

It should also be mentioned that, according to our computation, privately-owned real estate in the United States which qualifies for local tax-exemption as some kind of "charity" has a total assessed valuation of about $54 billion; which means that its true or cash value approximates $135 billions—a truly staggering sum, constituting nearly 12% of the total. Of this, nearly $80 billion or 60% is owned by religious organizations.

We note also in TABLE XXXIV that, according to our extrapolated computation, the true value of real estate in the United States (even while excluding certain categories) totals $1.14 trillion, of which more than $325 billion, or 28.5%, is exempt. This figure is actually too low, since it excludes *all* District federal property from our base for determining national totals: and there is considerable property of this kind in every city. Making proper allowance for this, we find that the true proportion would be approximately 31%, which is almost the same as that given in the article published in *Christianity Today*.

If we assume that the average ad valorem property tax is now 50 mills of assessed valuation and 20 mills of true value, we come up with the following results: all exempt property in the United States is now escaping an annual tax-levy of $7 billion, which averages about $140 for every family; the private-exempt, is escaping $2.7 billion, or $54 for each family; religious organizations alone are avoiding levies of $1.6 billion, or $32 for every family in the nation. This is what these exemptions are costing the American people at this time. And this takes no account of income-tax exemptions, which might equal or exceed the standard levies on real estate. If the exempt properties of the Catholic Church alone were to be taxed like other real estate, the levy would total about $1 billion in the U.S.

Finally, we should bear in mind that all categories of exempt property, which now total at least 30% of the total, are growing at an alarming rate and may, in the reasonable future, become 40 or 50%. When this has come to pass, the burden upon residential and business property will have become oppressive to the point of desperation.

51

Part Two:

CHURCHES AND THE FEDERAL INCOME TAX

CHAPTER VII:

PREFERENCES
AND IMMUNITIES

The immemorial privilege. The property-tax exemptions now accorded religious, educational, charitable, scientific, and many other non-profit organizations are so well established that few question them; but the benefits which these receive under the Internal Revenue Code belong in a different category.

It is true that religious bodies and officials have enjoyed special rights and privileges in many cultures since the beginning of history. For thousands of years, the Osirian priesthood in Egypt owned one third of the land, which always remained inviolable;[1] and all revenues and production therefrom were tax-free. The laws of Ezra specifically forbade the levying of any taxes, tolls, tributes, or customs upon any priest or Levite.[2] The Brahmana priesthood of India enjoyed even greater privileges and exemptions.[3] And when the Catholic Church achieved full primacy under Constantine the Great after 325, its hierarchy demanded and obtained extraordinary immunities, incomes, political power, and institutional advantages.[4]

A multitude of exemptions. The United States Department of Commerce publishes what is known as The Cumulative Index of organizations which are exempt from federal taxes on the contributions which they receive from their members, the public, and various other sources and which may be deducted from their own income by the donors. This list contains thousands of names, and in many cases these are simply categories which cover multitudes of subsidiary bodies. For example, a single line lists the Baptist Church and Its Related Institutions and therefore covers more than 90,000 individual congregations and organizations. No one knows how many tax-exempt bodies exist in the United States—there are hundreds of thousands; for almost any charitable, religious, educational, scientific, health, or welfare organization can qualify.

The most important general division among tax-exempt institutions consists, of course, of religious organizations, which are of great variety. The principal categories are churches, hospitals, and educational establishments; but there is, in addition, a vast complex of church-related and other "non-profit" enterprises which are also tax-exempt. Under the 1954 Internal Revenue Code, a taxpayer may deduct up to 30% of taxable income if he limits his contributions to churches, hospitals, and educational institutions; but if he scatters his largesse among a broader variety of recipients, he may deduct only 20%.[5]

The priest, the religious, and the minister. Since different treatment is accorded various religious functionaries under the Code, it is necessary to divide these into categories: (1) Catholic priests who are members of religious orders; (2) the "secular" Catholic clergy; (3) the personnel of non-sacerdotal Catholic religious orders; and (4) other clericals, such as rabbis, Protestant ministers, Ethical Culture leaders, etc. A Catholic priest—whether secular or religious—is a sacerdotal functionary who may hear confession, perform marriages, celebrate Mass, and administer other sacraments; members of non-sacerdotal orders are nuns or brothers known as the religious, who wear a distinctive garb and perform specific duties, such as teaching, and have taken the vows of celibacy, obedience, and poverty. Secular Catholic priests may own property and receive private income, but religious priests cannot, since they have taken the vow of poverty, a condition which applies also to all nuns and brothers.

Since all members of Catholic religious orders have taken the vow of poverty, they turn over any property or income they may have to their organizations and receive their maintenance in return; they are said in all cases to have no personal income and therefore they pay neither Social Security nor income tax levies nor do they file any reports. Approximately one half of the parish priests, assistants, bishops, archbishops, and cardinals in the United States belong in this category. However, a considerable number of these clerics are known as secular priests; but even they are exempt from the payment of income taxes on any cost necessary for the maintenance of their rectories or any activity performed in the service of their parishioners. If, however, they have personal income, they are supposed to report and pay taxes on this; but, since these priests handle large amounts of cash which they deposit in personal accounts, it must be virtually impossible to separate their private funds from those of the church, especially since the latter makes no accounting of its financial operations either to the Department of Internal Revenue or to its own constituents.

The bishop, archbishop, or cardinal who is the head of a diocese and who is empowered as a *corporation sole* to hold unlimited quantities of all types of wealth in his own name, belongs in a special category. He can "own" billions of dollars in real estate and intangible property and the Department of Internal Revenue says that, since he is an agent of the Church, he is to be treated as if he had assumed its identity. He makes no reports concerning these financial operations.

Furthermore, the Code specifically provides that lodging, and, in some cases, even the meals received by an employee are, under certain conditions, tax-exempt; but this applies only if these are "furnished to him by his employer for the convenience of the employer" and if "the meals are furnished on the business premises of the employer." [6] Since the church and rectory are the business premises of the employer and since it is for its convenience that its employees take their meals there, any cost involved in their preparation is exempt from income taxes for the recipients. And, since the cost of any garb essential for employment, and the transportation necessary to carry on that activity, are also tax-exempt, it is hard to see what taxable income any functionary of the Catholic Church is likely to have, especially since he may accumulate unlimited quantities of untaxed wealth in the form of personal gifts and donations. The practical result is that, according to the interpretations placed upon the Code by the Department of Internal Revenue, not only members of Catholic religious orders but also their secular clergy are excused from all Social Security and income taxes. The practical results of this ruling are sufficiently astounding. Let us see how it operates.

57

For example, a nun, garbed or not, may teach in a tax-supported school at a standard salary of, say, six or eight thousand dollars a year. No Social Security or withholding taxes are deducted from her pay; nor does she file any tax return. Let us go a step further: a Jesuit priest could conceivably serve as a bank president or a corporation executive at a salary of a hundred thousand or a million dollars a year, and he would neither pay any taxes nor report his income to any government agency.

In the District of Columbia, the Catholic bishop of the Washington archdiocese lives in a house assessed in 1964 at $193,993; and, since most church property is assessed at about one third of its true value, this prelate occupies a dwelling worth approximately $600,000. He could have a dozen cars in his garage; a household of fifty, who are considered, not his own, but the servants of the Church; and a living standard that a business man with a million-dollar income before taxes could not sustain. In addition, he may have several million dollars deposited in banks under his personal control and disposition. Nevertheless, the Department of Internal Revenue may declare that this personage has neither income nor property; and that, therefore, he need pay no taxes nor file any report. In addition, of course, his episcopal mansion is exempt from local property taxes since it is owned by the Church, even though the title to it is recorded in the name of the bishop who occupies it, as is all diocesan property, through the legal fiction of the *corporation sole*. The rabbi or minister who occupies his own house must pay local property taxes in full.

There is, however, an obscure ruling in the Code by which even rabbis and Protestant ministers can profit substantially: for it states that the gross income "of a minister of the Gospel" shall not include "the rental allowance paid to him as part of his compensation, to the extent used by him to rent or provide a home."[7] This has been interpreted to mean that any expense incurred by him in connection with his home, including utilities, repairs, decorating, linens, towels, furnishings, carpeting, furniture, etc., etc., with the exception only of food or personal servants, is tax-deductible; and that, with a short-term contract or mortgage, he may, by making proper arrangements with his congregation and by deducting all interest and principal payments, avoid income taxes altogether, although he must still file a return. When the contract is fulfilled or the mortgage liquidated, he is at liberty to repeat the process and thus avoid all income taxes during the period of his ministry. The same rules apply also upon retirement.

We should note also that no church or synagogue pays or deducts any Social Security or income tax levies on the salaries paid to rabbis or ministers; and these clerics, who are regarded as "self-employed," constitute the only group which may elect or reject participation in this program. In addition, they are also permitted to deduct not only their itemized deductions but also the standard 10% exemption from their incomes.

How much exempt property? Real estate belonging to any government agency, or to a church, a religious order, a school, nunnery, monastery, retreat, seminary, college, university, etc., or to a hospital, cemetery, charitable enterprise, or a religious or scientific publishing house is normally free from local property taxation. In many typical large cities, such church or church-related property now totals 10% of all real estate, 25 per cent or more of the exempt portion, and from 50 to 70 per cent of the exempt portion which is privately owned. For example, in the District of Columbia, it comprises 9% of all taxable property, 32% of all non-federal exempt real estate, and 55% of all private and exempt.[8] In Buffalo, such property is 7.4% of the taxable, 14% of all exempt, and 71% of all private and exempt classified as charitable.[9] Furthermore, the exempt portion is growing constantly: for example, in Buffalo, it was only 19% of the taxable in 1930; but in 1964 it constituted 44.2%.[10] TABLE XXXIV establishes that in the four cities, exempt property comprised 33.41% of the total; and that, omitting the District Federal, the exempt was 21.9%; the private-exempt 9.22%; and the religious was 5.46% of the total. Even more significant is the fact (Cf. TABLE XXXII) that religious property constituted 24.78% of all exempt; and 58.66% of the private-exempt.

The vanishing wealth. Many may be amazed to learn that churches and other "non-profit" organizations have enormous tax-exempt revenues identical to those on which individuals and corporations pay huge levies to state and federal authorities. There are also some 46,000 tax-exempt foundations in the United

States, many of which were created for the specific purpose of avoiding the inheritance tax and which continue to do business precisely as when they were privately owned, except that they are now required to convey their entire net income to other tax-exempt institutions; and such funds, to a very large extent, are channeled into the coffers of religious denominations or church-related enterprises, where they disappear completely and forever from all government scrutiny, and may be used for a multitude of commercial investments.

Unrelated business income. Any organization which can qualify for exemption from local property taxes, as well as any other non-profit corporation, is *exempt from taxation on income derived from interest, dividends, royalties, rent, or capital gains.* However, except in the case of churches, such unrelated business income must be reported on Form 990 so that the Department of Internal Revenue will at least be apprized of its nature and extent. This means, for example, that a charitable institution or a fraternal organization may purchase real estate, such as an apartment house, a shopping center, or an office building, finance the purchase either through a mortgage or a long-term contract, and collect the rents directly, which will be non-taxable. Or it can purchase any of those properties or a hotel or a factory and lease it to the original owner or anyone else. The rental paid on this lease is then deductible to the current operator, who continues to pay the taxes and run the business; the rentals collected by the tax-exempt organization, though reportable, are non-taxable; and thus, in something like twenty years the property may be owned outright by the tax-exempt entity without risking a single dollar; and the original seller may convert his property into cash with only a minor obligation. The money thus saved in unpaid taxes in twenty years will, under normal circumstances, exceed the value of the property. Under certain conditions, the property may also be removed from the local tax rolls, so that other citizens will, in effect, be contributing in double measure to the wealth thus accumulated by both parties to the sale and leaseback.

Non-sacerdotal business taxes. If, however, any tax-exempt body, *except a church or a sacerdotal order,* operates a business which gives service, like a hotel or a drug store, or engages in production or manufacture of any kind, then on any income derived from this, it must file a return on Form 990T and pay federal taxes on profits so obtained. For example, if a fraternal or non-sacerdotal religious order owns and operates a motel or a restaurant which caters to the public or a concern which manufactures greeting cards, carpets, wine, or anything else, the organization, as a corporate body, must report this activity and pay taxes on its profits. This is the reason why the Christian Brothers must pay income taxes on the profits from their business in Napa, California.

Tax-free investments. Because of the unique tax advantages which now exist, a great number of non-profit organizations are turning to property investments which they can make with very little and sometimes with no actual outlay of cash. The end of this activity is nowhere in sight: in fact, it is probably in its infancy. In a few decades most of the commercial property of the United States could very well be owned by tax-exempt organizations, who would pay no taxes on the income derived from these fabulous investments. It is also worth noting that no examination of the local tax-records is likely to reveal the true ownership of such property; for the current operator will generally appear as the taxpayer of record. In many cases, no entry will have been made in the county records at all: the whole transaction may have been consummated by an unrecorded contract and lease.

The unique tax-immunities. Among all tax-exempt bodies, churches (or an "association of churches"), occupy a special position under the Internal Revenue Code;[11] for they alone are exempt, not only from income taxes, but also from making any reports, no matter what their economic activities may be. The whole question of tax-exempt organizations and their "unrelated business income" receives extensive treatment in the Code.[12]

The quondam American ideal that the sole activity of churches should consist of religious worship supported by the voluntary contributions of their members has today sometimes been replaced by a philosophy which is capable of transforming them into vast financial empires, enjoying a variety of tax preferences which, if conferred upon a private corporation, would soon enable it to drive all competition into bankruptcy.

There are three principal sources from which a church, an

61

association of churches, or a sacerdotal order can derive such revenue and enjoy such immunity:

(1) As with other tax-exempt bodies, all income from interest, dividends, royalties, real estate rentals, capital gains, or gifts from tax-free foundations is exempt. However, even if a religious body is the sole or principal owner of any corporation engaged in manufacture or service, the corporation itself must file reports and pay taxes like any other. The prime stockholder, however, pays no taxes and makes no reports; and it can manipulate the corporation for its own benefit by placing its own personnel in key positions. If it is the sole owner of a manufacturing corporation, for example, it can easily make preferential sales; if the business is a hotel or a chain of motels, it can favor its own people with free or cut-rate accommodations.

(2) Any tax-exempt body may set up what is known as a "feeder corporation";[13] and if the income from this consists of rentals, interest, or dividends, these will be non-taxable to the parent only. However, if the parent-body is a church or a sacerdotal order; if it receives the entire income; if the "feeder" is a corportation engaged solely in the construction, purchase, sale, or operation of rental property; if the holdings are without encumbrance; and if there are no leases exceeding five years, then not only the parent, but also the corporation itself, are both relieved of federal reports and taxation. In short, a church or a priestly order is permitted to set up a feeder corporation under an assumed name, construct apartments, shopping centers, office buildings, retirement communities, etc., and the government cannot levy taxes on, or even demand any information concerning, the income from these projects or the activities of the corporation itself.

(3) There is one more great category of unrelated business income which only churches and sacerdotal orders can enjoy without the imposition of taxes or reports; and this is derived from enterprises wholly owned and directly operated by them. For example, a church can own and operate hotels, stores, mines, newspapers, farms, industries of every kind and description; and, no matter how great the profits, no taxes will be paid nor need any reports be filed. A sacerdotal order, such as the Franciscans

62

or the Jesuits, can own and operate radio stations, public utilities, office buildings, race tracks, distilleries, etc., and no reports of any kind will be required by any legal authority. A church can own and operate a restaurant, hotel, drug store, daily newspaper, or cattle ranch with complete immunity. Under certain conditions a church organization can take over a private enterprise; and, while operating it for profit, qualify *this* as a charitable institution and thus become exempt from local property taxes also. For example, a church might acquire a luxury hotel, and use it as a retirement home for its personnel and it would be removed from the rolls of taxable property on the ground that it had been transformed into a charity. Or it might acquire a nursing home catering to the general public and have this qualify as such an institution.

Communicants also in the dark. We note also that not only is the government without information concerning the financial operations of various churches and sacerdotal orders: the contributing members of these organizations are equally in the dark. Only occasionally does the public, by accident or otherwise, learn of these activities; and then they sometimes make headline news. It is certain that the unrelated business income of churches is far greater than any one knows. Only a stringent federal law could bring all these operations into the light of day.

A burning issue. A congressional committee headed by the honorable Wright Patman of Texas is now endeavoring to compel all tax-free foundations to pay income taxes as do ordinary corporations; should he be successful, it would seem no more than fair that all churches also disclose their unrelated business income and pay taxes on profits derived therefrom; and certainly on that obtained from the operation of any competitive business.

Since churches and sacerdotal orders enjoy such unique immunities, privileges, and exemptions under existing law, their economic activities are of vital concern to everyone. And, since they make no reports concerning their incomes, holdings, profits, or accumulations, neither the government nor any one else can make an accurate estimate of these, either as to their present extent or their growth in recent years. That both are enormous is certain; and future developments will not only affect drastically the relationship between church and state but also the economic position of every human being in the United States.

It should be obvious that there is no essential difference between outright cash subsidies and preferential tax-treatment for an activity which operates in competition with normal tax-paying business and which is in no way related to any act of religious worship. Any church which profits by such an advantage has become a partner or a favored ward of the state and has effectively breached the classic Jeffersonian "Wall of Separation." Any law which gives such preferential treatment to a church-body is one "respecting an establishment of religion" and is outlawed in the First Amendment to our Constitution.

CHAPTER VIII:

RELIGIOUS TAX-EXEMPTIONS
IN PRACTICE

The threat. The nature and extent of the income tax immunities enjoyed by religious organizations and functionaries and their potential effect upon our culture and economy are indeed breathtaking. Thirty years ago, the federal income tax was only an irritant; but today it has become the most important single economic element in American life. And one reason why both property and income taxes are so heavy is that foundations, churches, and church-affiliated organizations enjoy the unique tax-immunities described in the preceding chapter. Dr. Eugene Carson Blake, former president of the National Council of Churches, has stated: "In view of their favored tax position, with reasonably good management, America's churches ought to be able to control the whole economy of the nation within the predictable future." [1]

The growing exemptions. We have seen that in the District of Columbia nearly 46% of all property assessments were exempt in 1964, partly because of the federal installations there.[2] But even in such a typical and conventional city as Buffalo, as we have pointed out, the ratio of exempt to taxable real estate increased from 19 to 44.2% in thirty-four years.[3] In Baltimore, exempt property was 28.86% of the taxable[4] and in Denver, which has not yet succumbed so deeply to this modern trend, it was 18.45%,[5] and growing rapidly. By far the greatest category of such holdings is the religious, which constituted 58.6% of all privately owned, exempt property belonging to non-profit organizations in the four cities covered by our analysis.[6]

The disparate burdens. Under the Internal Revenue Code, a

man and his wife, each earning $6,000 a year, made a combined payment of $348.00 in 1964 for Social Security (a sum matched by their employers) ; and, in addition to any levies exacted by the state, another $2,420 in federal income taxes—a total of $3,116. If their income rose to $24,000, this levy would be $8,001; if to $100,000, it would be $48,576. However, when such sums accrue to certain functionaries of the Catholic Church, there are no deductions, payments, or reports. Catholic chaplains in the armed forces who belong to religious orders pay neither Social Security nor income taxes; whereas all rabbis and Protestant ministers are subjected to income tax levies and may accept or reject participation in Social Security. According to the *Official Catholic Directory* of 1964, there were then in the U.S.A. 57,328 Catholic priests, 12,132 brothers, and 180,015 nuns, a total of 249,475 functionaries who have taken their final vows; in addition to which there were 48,750 seminarians.[7] The present living standards of all these could probably not be maintained at less than an average of $5,000 a year; and, since they pay no income taxes, they are escaping annual levies which could not be less than $200 million on similar incomes received by persons in secular occupations.

Business taxes. Employers must pay heavy state unemployment taxes; contribute to Social Security an amount equal to that paid by their employees; and must submit to a complex of other levies from the city, the county, the state, and the federal government. The federal corporation income tax alone is 50%; and if the owner of a corporate enterprise pays himself any dividends, he must first pay the corporation tax on this, and then the personal income tax to state and federal governments for any monies he receives from his own business either in the form of salary or dividends. The total of these various taxes may exceed 85% of all the profits of the business.

In many communities, the annual real estate tax approximates 4% of its total value and averages from 15 to 20% of the gross income derived from commercial investments; in most industries, income taxes, when added to all other government levies, consume from 50 to 70% of the net income. A reasonable estimate is that the average business pays to various government agencies a sum exceeding its total assets every ten years. But churches, even when they engage in the same kind of activity, are exempt from every kind of taxation.

Under existing law, any religious entity may set up a competitive enterprise, staff it with unsalaried religious personnel, and pay nothing—in some cases, not even the local ad valorem tax on business property. It is being done all over the United States.

No one knows the extent to which this ecclesiastical enterprise has already proceeded. Churches, it must be emphasized again, are not required to reveal investments or financial activities to anyone; and on this subject they tend to preserve a profound silence, especially to their own communicants. In a burst of candor, one Catholic spokesman stated: "I would love to see just one denomination spell out the tax-exempt properties it actually holds."[8]

The tax-free foundation. During the last two or three decades, another factor in the American economy has risen to great importance: viz., the tax-free business or non-profit foundation, which is required to convey its entire net income to other tax-exempt organizations or use it for "charitable" or similar purposes. A visit to the office of Congressman Wright Patman, who is investigating these foundations, revealed that in 1952 there were 26,000 and that now there are at least 46,000 of these, 546 of which, under intensive scrutiny in 1964, had an income of more than $1.4 billion from industrial stocks in 1960 compared to only $556 million in 1951.[9] With the Ford Foundation at the head, which has wealth exceeding $2 billion at book value, they now have assets of more than $16.3 billion.[10] In addition to their business income, these foundations received gifts from taxpayers totalling $8.2 billion in 1960, all of which was deductible by their donors from their taxable income and constituted an annual loss of $2.8 billion to the federal government. The combined income of the tax-free foundations now exceeds $11 billion a year. While all of this is immune from state and federal levies, reports are required and the Treasury Department can at least obtain some knowledge concerning the extent and disposition of the money. By permitting the establishment of these tax-exempt foundations, the government has already lost far more than if it had abolished the Estate and Inheritance Tax forty years ago; and these losses will grow progressively in the future. Every one is a loser except the tax-exempt bodies who receive the money given away by the foundations.

All this is of vital importance in the field of church-state relations. Approximately half of all the money received by tax-free foundations is paid over to churches and other religious organizations; the rest goes to educational, health, and welfare foundations, a great many of which are church-related or controlled. It is therefore certain that well over $6 or even $8 billion every year flows from the foundations into the coffers of churches and their subsidiaries.[11] What happens to this money beyond that point cannot be ascertained, since no church or sacerdotal order is required to render any reports. Such funds can be invested in a multitude of business enterprises, which, in turn, are immune from taxes or government scrutiny.

The Mormon Church. The known business, industrial, and other investment holdings of churches and church-related institutions today run into untold billions of dollars in the United States. In part at least because of its highly centralized control, the Church of Jesus Christ of Latter Day Saints (Mormon) has been remarkably successful in this field. It owns stocks, bonds, hotels, farms, a sugar refinery, book and department stores, mines, publishing houses, restaurants, TV stations, newspapers, banks, and large tracts of land. It owns and operates hundreds of so-called welfare farms, one of which, located in Florida, has 740,000 acres and more than 100,000 cattle. It recently purchased 786 acres and fourteen commercial buildings in an expanding area of Salt Lake City, to be held for investment and development.[12] Any one visiting there in 1964 could see that fourteen stories were being added to the Church-owned Utah Hotel, which, together with the huge commercial building announced by President David McKay in October, 1960, comprises a $40 million construction project. A similar office structure is under way in New York City also. The Church has invested $1.5 million in a center of Polynesian culture in Hawaii, where nightly shows attract large crowds of tourists.[13] It is common knowledge that it owns controlling stock in the Union Pacific Railway. Former Governor J. Bracken Lee of Utah made the statement a few years ago that the income of the Church was at least $1 million a day;[14] but when pressed for proof, he admitted that this was only an estimate—and it was probably a very conservative one. Only the highest officials of the Church have any definite knowledge concerning the wealth, income, and economic complex which constitutes the Church of Jesus Christ of Latter Day Saints. It prides itself on paying the local real estate taxes on its commercial property; but it is certain that it is not required to pay any state or federal income levies.

Protestants in business. Churches belonging specifically to the Protestant tradition have also taken advantage of the existing tax-immunities; and their business activities are more likely to be publicized, since they are almost certainly known to the membership. For example, in 1954, the First Baptist, First Christian, and Second Presbyterian churches of Bloomington, Illinois, acting as a syndicate, and using $200,000 advanced by some of their own members, bought from Hilton Hotels, Inc., the 435-room Biltmore Hotel in Dayton, Ohio, for $3.5 million; the transaction was financed by mortgages of $3.3 million, which required interest and principal payments of approximately $225,000 a year. The property was then leased back at $250,000 to the former owner, which assumed complete responsibility for taxes, insurance, repairs, operation, etc. The churches had recovered the original investment and were paying themselves almost $8,500 each annually when, in 1963, they sold the hotel back to the original owner with a tax-free capital gain of $450,000.[15]

How is it done? To analyze the *modus operandi* of such a transaction is most informative. Let us assume that a man or a corporation has owned a hotel, apartment house, or office building, now worth a million dollars, for fifteen or twenty years, during which the depreciation, which is always a major financial consideration, has been almost exhausted. When this is the case, the owner must pay full federal taxes on all net operating revenue, which means that the annual profit is reduced by $50,000; in twenty years this totals a million dollars and means a difference of $500,000 in net income. The project is therefore sold to a tax-exempt organization and the capital gains tax, which may come to about $150,000, is paid. The seller takes a down payment of perhaps $100,000 and obtains $900,000 through

69

mortgage financing. He then has $850,000 of free capital for use elsewhere, which he can double in less than ten years, *before taxes*. He then leases back the hotel at, say $75,000 a year, all of which (in addition to taxes, insurance, repairs, etc.) is deductible. The church will amortize the 5% mortgage at $59,640 a year in 25 years or at $67,360 in 20, at the end of which it will own the property free and clear. In the meantime, it has recovered not only the original investment, but also another $52,800 in twenty years or $284,075 in twenty-five. When the mortgage is liquidated, the church has a tax-exempt income of $75,000 a year without having one penny invested or ever having lifted a finger to give any service. Or the former owner may now repurchase the property for $1 million (which will be a tax-free capital gain to the church) and repeat the process of depreciation. In twenty years, the tax-exempt organization will have a net profit of $1,300,000; and the former owner will have a cash advantage through tax-avoidance of approximately $500,000. Thus the government will lose approximately $1 million of revenue as a result of a deal which involved only that amount in the first place, almost all of which was borrowed.

Some specific cases. It is therefore not strange that many churches are engaging in this wonderful game of purchase-lease-back-and-resale. In downtown Los Angeles, the Temple Baptist Church owns the entire stock in the Auditorium Company, valued at several millions. This pays partial taxes on the realty, but none on the business income; and if the corporation itself is free from encumbrance, it too can qualify for income tax exemption. The First Methodist Church of Chicago owns and worships in the Chicago Temple, a 22-story Loop structure, now worth at least $6 million. This church also pays partial property taxes, assessed against space rented commercially; but it pays no income taxes on its rentals, which amount to about $250,000 a year.

In 1954, Wesleyan University of Illinois bought the Roosevelt Hotel in Hollywood and the El Rancho in Sacramento for $10 million, financed by a down payment of $200,000 and mortgages of $9.8 million. Since, under a special ruling of the Department of Internal Revenue, an educational institution may operate a business tax-free for five years, the University held the hotels for this period, made an interim operating profit, and then, for $700,000, sold its equity to the Catholic St. Andrew's parish in Chicago, which now holds and operates them indefinitely as a tax-free income.[16]

Religion in business. A Presbyterian church in Ohio operates a cinder block business;[17] the Seventh-Day Adventists operate a multi-million-dollar vegetarian food industry, known as the Loma Linda Food Company of California;[18] the Southern Baptist Board bought Burlington Mills of Cheraw, South Carolina, for $2.9 million and leased it back to the firm at rentals which will liquidate the debt in twenty years;[19] the Baptist Foundation of Texas does a large business in leasebacks at a profit of at least 20% on the investments;[20] and an obscure sect known as the Self-Realization Fellowship is doing a very lucrative business with two restaurants in California.[21] On November 10, 1964, the Muskingum Presbytery, with headquarters at Beverly, Ohio, purchased the Superlite Builders Supply, a huge cement-block manufacturing company, in Phoenix, Arizona.[22] Similar undertakings are prospering in a thousand places under the benign protection of preferential tax laws.

Local assessors seeking more revenue have not been very successful in attempts to place religiously owned property under taxation. In a case appealed from Rhode Island, the Supreme Court ruled, April 16, 1962, that the individual states have full authority to determine all local questions relating to the taxation or exemption of church property. When the District of Columbia attempted to tax the property of the Catholic Education Press, the publishing arm of the Catholic University of America, it was overruled by the Supreme Court on July 3, 1952, on the ground that the Press was a scientific institution. In 1959, the city of Nashville placed valuations on the publishing houses of the Methodist and Baptist denominations located in that city and attempted to collect the levies assessed against them; however, in the words of the *Wall Street Journal,* "All it won was an agreement putting on the tax-rolls a cafeteria, some parking lots and vending machines used by employees of the church publications."[23]

The Catholic colossus. The tax-immunities and exempt business properties and income of Protestant churches are indeed

71

extensive; but they pale into insignificance when compared to those of the Catholic hierarchy, which not only admits but openly boasts of its enormous wealth. In the words of an official spokesman, Father Richard Grider, as reported in *The Wall Street Journal,* it "must be the biggest corporation in the United States . . ."[24] It is indeed: in comparison, such financial complexes as Ford or even General Motors sink into insignificance.

The National Council of Christians and Jews has estimated the current assets of all charitable institutions, including the churches, at $54.8 billion, which is an increase of 170% in the last 20 years; and it predicts that the total will be $100 billion by 1975.[25] However, this study has already demonstrated[26] not only that this estimate is far too low but also that by 1975, if present trends continue, the Catholic Church will probably own 75% of the religious portion of this wealth; and that the latter comprised almost 60% of all the "charitable" property in 1964. And, we might add, it is at least possible that the intangible investments of the Vatican in the United States may exceed in value the real estate it possesses in this country.

The Knights of Columbus. These make up a fraternal order which, in various ways, parallels the Masonic, and has, since its organization in 1882, grown greatly in wealth and influence. On June 30, 1960, the Knights officially declared their assets to be $162,928,575.[27] Since then, these have swollen to more than $200 million, including department stores, warehouses, and a steel mill.[28] The K. of C. have contributed half a million dollars for scholarships at the Catholic University of America; a huge sum for a radio transmitter at the Vatican; and, among other denominational gifts, $1,150,000 to construct the 329-foot campanile at the Shrine of the Immaculate Conception.[29] The order spends large sums for advertising in national magazines intended to win converts for the Church. All the activities carried on have only one purpose: to strengthen the position and extend the power of the Vatican.

One recent transaction which involved the Knights deserves a special note. In a three-cornered deal, a Chicago broker bought Yankee Stadium in 1953 through financed loans of $6.9 million; he sold the *land* to the Knights, leasing it back at an annual rental of $182,000; he then leased land *and* structures back to the ball club.[30] Since the depreciation had probably been nearly exhausted, this was an extremely lucrative transaction all around (except, of course, for the government), too complicated to describe here in detail. The only really pertinent fact is that in twenty-four years the overall result will be that the various taxing authorities will lose several million dollars in revenue.

Alcohol and religion. One of the most interesting cases involving tax-exemption is that of the Christian Brothers, who operate a multi-million-dollar winery and distillery at Napa, California, which, as a church-related enterprise, had enjoyed complete federal tax-exemption on the vast profits derived from its sales. Taken to court, the Brothers, under protest, paid a levy of $489,000. When their appeal was finally settled in Sacramento under Judge Halbert, July 24, 1961, a signal victory was won for the separation of church and state; for they were forced to pay an additional $3,477,390 in back taxes and to make subsequent payments like any other corporation for profit.[31] This decision was based on certain 1950 revisions in the Revenue Code which provide that if any tax-exempt body, *except a church or a sacerdotal order,* engages in manufacture, production, sale, or service to the public for profit, it must report this activity on form 990 T and pay federal taxes on the net income derived therefrom.[32] However, had this enterprise been operated by the Franciscans, the Benedictines, the Dominicans, or the Jesuits, they would have been immune.

Their name is legion. In this relationship, it is pertinent to add that considerable laxity seems to exist in the enforcement of existing law, for a great many similar enterprises are flourishing among non-sacerdotal bodies without any known imposition of taxes. For example, we have the following, which are heavily advertised in the secular press, sold in quantities to the general public, all free from taxes: fruit cakes, hams, bacon, and sausages, produced by the Trappist monks near Bardstown, Kentucky; preserves and jellies (more than 3 million jars a year) made and packed by monks of the same order at Spencer, and candies produced by Trappistine nuns at Trentham, Massachusetts; beef from St. Benedict's Abbey, Aspen, Colorado; St. Peter's fishing lures, made and blessed by cloistered nuns at Canton, Ohio; monk's bread, baked and sold by Trappists at Collegeville,

73

Minnesota; and oranges from the Abbey of St. Leo, Florida. At Walls, Mass., a priest has forty-four nuns who have produced between four and five million icons of Mary, placed by pious Catholic motorists for safety in their cars: this business nets $150,000 a year.[33] All of these and countless similar industries are not only exempt from Social Security, unemployment, intangible, and income taxes, but in many cases from real estate levies also.

In Boston, the Catholic Church purchased Loew's, the second largest theater in the state, and changed its name to the Donnelly Memorial;[34] and, under the pretext that it is used for Church conventions and the showing of religious films, this has doubtless been granted exemption from local property taxes by friendly assessors.

A few years ago, the Catholic Church purchased a 500-room hotel in Detroit, Michigan, to be used as a home for retired priests and religious. Even though the facility continued to house commercial guests and to serve the public in its restaurants, a lenient city council, which counted eight Catholics among its nine members, granted the property full tax immunity as a religious charity.[35]

A chain of 22 Massachusetts nursing homes, 10 of them in Boston, was recently purchased for $4.7 million by the Roman Catholic diocese of Austin, Texas, and leased back to the original owners, Geriatrics Management. The terms of the sale provide that payments will be completed in 15 years, entirely out of income; however, this period may be prolonged if profits are less than anticipated. It is reported, we read, that great numbers of other business concerns are contemplating similar lucrative, tax-avoiding arrangements.[36]

Religion and real estate. The Potomac Plaza, as we have already noted, is a large apartment project already built in the District of Columbia and owned by the Catholic Church through a subsidiary corporation. We have mentioned that the Società Generale Immobiliere is now constructing the Watergate Project[37] at the approximate cost of $70 million.[38] It has also been reported that the same corporation will construct a great hotel and office center in Montreal, involving an investment of about $400 million. It is quite possible that in such a predominantly

Catholic community, this will be immune, not only from income, but also from local property taxes.

The soldiers of Jesus. However, the business enterprises of all other churches or tax-exempt organizations fade into insignificance when compared to the activities of the Society of Jesus. These canny and far-sighted priests are without peer or parallel in the realm of finance.

Unlike the Christian Brothers, the Jesuits are sacerdotal: Loyola University in New Orleans is therefore permitted, under our Internal Revenue Code, to operate radio-TV stations WML and WWL with complete immunity from taxation or government scrutiny. If this were done by any Protestant or other private educational institution in America as now organized, the business could not escape the payment of income taxes. This communications facility is therefore able to undersell its competitors, even while making fabulous but unrevealed profits.

Revelations from Germany. We are indebted to the popular and politically potent German weekly, *Der Spiegel,* for important information concerning the economic dealings of the Vatican, and particularly of the Jesuits in the United States. In two articles,[39] this publication delineates the astonishing operations which radiate from Vatican City. The most influential directors of this vast financial empire have been members of papal families, including Marcantonio and Giulio Pacelli, nephews of Pope Pius XII, and Count Stanislaus Pecci, great nephew of Pope Leo XIII, who died in 1903.

The second article states that the Vatican is today probably the world's largest shareholder in corporate wealth. However, the most space is devoted to the financial operations of the Jesuits; and it tells in detail how, for generations, they have controlled international banking systems, the principal factories of various nations, and especially the munitions industries, out of which they have accumulated vast fortunes by selling arms to various combatants. It is indeed an amazing story.

A mine of gold. The author deals at some length with the activities of the Jesuits in the United States. "The entrance of the Society of Jesus," he declares, "into the world of American finance first became evident about fifty years ago when the Italian financier, A. P. Giannini, founded the Bank of California"

75

(originally called the Bank of Italy), "which is today known as the Bank of America, and which is one of the world's largest banks." (It is actually the largest.) "Giannini was really nothing more than an agent for the Jesuits, since they supplied him with his original capital. Today, the Order owns 51% of the stock in the Bank of America."

A kingdom of bananas. The article states further that the Jesuits own controlling interest in the Di Georgio Fruit Company, which, as an American corporation, owns several processing plants and vast citrus groves in California and Florida; but which, as an international cartel, owns more than a hundred steamships and many of the banana plantations in Central America, which, in turn, exercise great influence over governments existing there. *Der Spiegel* adds that the Jesuits also own controlling stock in the Phillips Petroleum Corporation and the Creole Petroleum Company, which owns vast oil concessions in South America.

The Bank of America currently pays dividends of about $60 million a year and its stock had a market value of well over $2 billion in 1964. Phillips Petroleum disburses nearly $100 million a year to its stockholders and its securities have a market value of nearly $2.5 billion. The Creole Petroleum Company has outstanding stock with a market value (as of 1964) of nearly $4 billion and its annual dividends total almost $200 million. From these three sources alone, therefore, the American Jesuits have a reputed income of nearly $180 million a year from holdings with a current market value exceeding $4 billion.

An industrial empire. But this is by no means all. For, according to *Der Spiegel,* the Society of Jesus is also a heavy investor in both Republic and National Steel and in the four greatest aircraft manufacturing companies in the United States, namely Boeing, Lockheed, Douglas, and Curtis-Wright. The common stocks of these six industrial giants had a combined 1964 market value of about $5 billion; and they paid annual dividends of nearly $200 million.

Assuming that this information is authentic, the Society of Jesus has an American portfolio with a market value of not less than $6 billion and an annual income of about $250 million. In addition, the Society undoubtedly has a great variety of other investments in the United States, where it is a comparative new-comer. In Europe, the Society has been extending its control over a vast network of commercial enterprises for centuries; and, as *Der Spiegel* points out, has always remained more or less independent of the Vatican.

Who supports the Vatican? There is one more exceedingly significant statement in the article: "The eight thousand priests who belong to the Order in America can always count on the cooperation of the Roman authorities, because the American bishops are on their side. And their position with the Roman Curia is powerful indeed: and this is so because the Vatican receives more money every year from the New York archdiocese alone than it does from all the Catholics in Europe combined."

Since only 4% of American Catholics reside in the New York archdiocese, this means (if all American Catholics contribute at the same rate) that at least 95% of all Vatican revenues come from the United States. It would be interesting indeed to know just how much cash flows across the Atlantic in this golden river; and also the extent to which this has contributed to the depletion of our gold reserves. It is possible that the Vatican drains this country of from $2 to $3 billion every year, or between $6 and $8 million during every twenty-four hour period.

Who can compete? In closing, let us recall the words of *Christianity Today*:[40] "Consider the facts," it warns. "A good business earns six per cent after taxes. Exempt from such taxes, a church could profit twelve rather than six per cent. Since this higher return offers an attractive loan investment, the sponsoring church can borrow money at lower interest rates. If, for example, it borrows at four per cent to engage in business, the church can realize eight per cent on its investment.

"Suppose a church buys a million-dollar business that in view of tax-exemptions shows an annual profit of $120,000. It can borrow $800,000 to purchase the business at the preferred loan rate of four per cent, or $32,000. Hence, on an investment of $200,000, the church will net $88,000 or 44 per cent.

"Suppose, however, the net were only 25 per cent. An investment at 25 per cent compounded doubles in less than three years, quadruples in six, in thirty years will multiply itself one thousand times. Starting with a million dollars and encouraged by the present tax exemptions for religious bodies engaging in unrelated business activities, any church by this procedure, could own America in 60 years."

Must this be again? This being true, what is there to prevent the Catholics, the Mormons, or some really enterprising Protestant churches from increasing their commercial property holdings in geometrical ratio in the future? But if half or most of the wealth of this nation passes into their hands, who will support the government and the welfare state? And have we nothing in our future prospectus better than a Spanish Civil War, a French or a Russian Revolution, or a Mexican or a Cuban upheaval, to expropriate the lands and the investments of those who speak in the name of Him who had not where to lay his head?

Suggestions. In the following brief chapter, we offer some tentative suggestions as to what should be done in the United States in order to avoid the terrible disasters and upheavals which have overtaken countless previous cultures and which have been major causes in their destruction. It must be emphasized, however, that the remedies proposed are the author's own, and have not been officially proposed by Protestants and Other Americans United or, so far as we are aware, by any other national organization of importance. We simply state our own opinions and leave them to the consideration of the reader and the public.

CHAPTER IX:

* ## WHAT SHOULD BE DONE?

I. ALL PRIVATELY OWNED, EXEMPT PROPERTIES SHOULD SUBMIT VOLUNTARILY, AT LEAST TO PARTIAL TAXATION.

Since the pyramiding cost of government has made the tax-burden such an acute issue, it now seems only fair that all privately owned and operated educational, social, scientific, religious, and other "charitable" institutions should submit by their own volition to some form of property taxation, at least to the extent of reimbursing their communities for minimum services, such as the cost of roads, streets, sidewalks, sewers, and police and fire protection, without which they could not operate. If these and similar expenses constitute 25% of the ordinary tax-burden, it seems only equitable that assessments in that proportion should be placed on these properties.

Neither churches nor any other charitable organizations expect to receive water from the city or gas or electricity from the utility companies without charge: why should they expect other and equally important services at the expense of the community? They pay salaries to their employees and pay for supplies and furnishings; and they regularly meet a thousand other operational costs. If all Americans were members of churches, such taxation would cost them nothing, since it would reduce existing levies on homes and business property. If many have no such affiliation, it is unjust to burden them with expenses incurred by other private groups. Federal housing projects, for example, reimburse their communities for minimum services.

II. LIMITATIONS SHOULD BE PLACED ON EXEMPTIONS FROM INCOME TAXES.

All would probably agree with us that income received by any non-profit organization from its members or the public should be free from taxation, as long as the entity is voluntary, does not engage in any kind of business whatever, and exists to attain a common purpose, which unites the membership. However, such blanket immunity should apply only to voluntary contributions; revenue derived from interest, dividends, royalties, rentals, capital gains, tax-exempt foundations, or business operations of any kind should be taxed exactly as if it were received by private corporations for profit. Tax-free unrelated business incomes for churches and other private entities make the federal government a partner with them in all these undertakings and, at least in the case of churches, violate the first amendment to the Constitution.

III. SPECIAL TREATMENT FOR HOSPITALS AND EDUCATIONAL INSTITUTIONS.

Hospitals, scientific research institutions, non-profit and non-sectarian schools, etc., are in an entirely different category from a religious congregation, a debating society, or a fraternal order; and the tax laws should recognize this difference by permitting tax-free unrelated business income so long as it is used for operational, not capital, expenditures. However, full financial reports should be made to the government and to their contributors; and taxes should be paid on surplus income, as is done by a corporation for profit.

It should be emphasized that nothing here said should be interpreted to mean that churches and other tax-exempt groups should be forbidden to engage in business or to receive unrelated business income; we simply mean that their immunity to disclosure and their preferential tax-treatment should be altered or abolished.

IV. MEMBERS AND CONTRIBUTORS SHOULD RE-CEIVE FINANCIAL REPORTS.

The right of any voluntary organization to receive tax-free contributions from its members and the public should carry a compensatory obligation: namely, to furnish all its members and contributors with a complete financial statement of all monies received and expended, of all surpluses or properties on hand, etc. Every municipal government publishes such a report for the general public; any person who owns a share of General Motors stock can require such an accounting from the corporation: why should not every member who has contributed to a voluntary organization have the same right?

Any voluntary association whose controlling officers refuse or fail to make such a report to their membership or who decline to open their books to such scrutiny should thereafter be required to pay full income taxes on all contributions received, as if they were net profit to a private corporation.

V. TITLE TO PROPERTIES OF TAX-FREE ORGANIZA-TIONS SHOULD BE VESTED IN A BOARD OF TRUSTEES RESPONSIBLE TO THE MEMBERSHIP.

The property owned by any private tax-exempt organization or association should be titled to a Board of Trustees responsible to its contributors or membership. Any property belonging to a voluntary organization, especially a church congregation, if not already so titled, should be conveyed to such a board, so responsible. Any organization which fails or refuses to comply should lose every form of tax-immunity.

VI. PRESENT DISCRIMINATION AND PERSONAL TAX-IMMUNITIES SHOULD BE ENDED.

There was a time when all salaries received by government employees were non-taxable. Not only was this favoritism abolished, but the principle was established that every form of secular income must be reported. For example, waitresses, taxi-drivers, and porters must report their tips. Rabbis and ministers would do society a great service by relinquishing the tax-advantages which most of them now enjoy; and they should insist that the Catholic priest who now occupies a million-dollar mansion, has a small army of personnel at his disposal who are actually his servants, and a fleet of expensive cars, report the full value of all this as personal income and pay taxes thereon in full. Nuns teaching in public schools and priests serving as chaplains should pay income taxes like any one else.

VII. ALL BUSINESS INCOME SHOULD BE TAXED.

Of far greater importance, however, are the tax-exempt business incomes enjoyed by churches and other exempt, voluntary organizations, derived from interest, dividends, rentals, mortgages, leases, capital gains, business operations, etc.: all of these should be taxed, exactly as if the recipients were private corporations for profit. And it is simply intolerable that a private order, like the Jesuits, should be permitted to own billions in intangible assets and receive hundreds of millions of dollars of business income annually without paying any taxes or even making any disclosure concerning it.

VIII. THERE SHOULD BE NO DIRECT OR INDIRECT GOVERNMENT SUBSIDY TO ANY RELIGIOUS ORGANIZATION.

The complete separation of Church and State must be maintained; and this means that no level of government should ever under any circumstances or to the smallest degree favor one church or any group of churches over another, or make any concession to all denominations collectively in any way, or institute any legislation which treats any or all such communions in any respect differently from any other purely private and voluntary organization. The State should neither discourage nor encourage the individual right to worship or not to worship in whatever manner each person may choose.

Perhaps the most burning issue before the American people

today is whether or not government aid shall be given to parochial and other church-related schools. Although the Lutherans have some 1,600 and the Seventh-Day Adventists 1,200 such institutions, *they* are not asking for tax-money: in fact, they are openly denouncing all such subsidies. The same is true of other Protestant and miscellaneous denominations, all of which take the position that if any church wishes to organize a school, it may do so, but it must establish acceptable academic standards and pay the entire cost of the project itself.

It so happens that virtually 100% of the pressure for public tax money to support religious schools comes from the Catholic hierarchy, which operates approximately 90% of all such institutions which exist in the United States. Let us contemplate the probable results, if the Roman bishops are given what they are now demanding: (1) in a short time, 12 or 15 million pupils may be receiving full-time, segregated indoctrination in Catholic schools at a cost to the public treasury of perhaps $10 billion or more a year; (2) there will, quite possibly, be a large number of conversions to Catholicism, which, combined with the prolific birth-rate among Catholics, could, in due course, place 25 million pupils in their sectarian schools; (3) such a development, financed largely by Protestants and other Americans, would transform the United States into a Catholic nation in less than 50 years; (4) in the meantime, most of the other large religious divisions, in sheer self-defense, would be compelled to set up their own parallel and competing sectarian schools; and, since there are nearly a hundred substantial denominations in the United States, we could expect a great number of parochial systems of education; (5) this would result in the fragmentation of our society into mutually suspicious and isolated groups, as has already happened in Holland, where the population is divided into (a) Catholics; (b) the Dutch Reformed; and (c) the Godless, as they are called, who still send their children to the rapidly shrinking non-sectarian schools; (6) this would effectively destroy our public school system together with the American way of life, in which people of every faith and ethnic origin may mingle on terms of friendship, equality, confidence, understanding, and reciprocal trust.

It is therefore mandatory that not one single dollar of public

83

money be given to any religious organization, to further its sectarian education or for any other activity of any kind whatsoever.

* * *

This, we believe, is the minimum program that should be adopted to insure the survival of the American republic.

APPENDIX

STATISTICAL TABLES

TABLE I—RELIGIOUS GROUPS IN FOUR CITIES[1]

City	Population	Jews	Catholics	Protestants, Etc.
Buffalo	528,000	19,200	200,000	120,000
Washington	760,000	45,000	80,500	225,000
Baltimore	939,000	66,000	200,000	250,000
Denver	495,000	17,000	90,000	140,000
TOTAL	2,722,000	147,200	570,500	735,800
Ratio to All Communicants		10.13%	39.25%	50.62%

[1] These statistics are taken from the tables which analyze the four cities individually.

TABLE II—COMPARABLE RELIGIOUS RATIOS[1]

Item	In United States	%	In Four Cities	%
Population	186,000,000	100	2,722,000	1.46
Churches	319,240	100	1,674	.52
Church Membership:		% of U.S. Population		% of Pop. in 4 Cities
Jewish	5,509,000	2.96	147,200	5.41
Catholic	43,847,938	23.57	570,500	20.95
Protestant, Etc.[2]	68,598,064	36.88	735,800	27.03
TOTAL	117,955,002	63.41	1,453,500	53.39
Enrollment in Catholic El. and Secon. Schools[3]	6,073,440		118,506	
Ratio to National			1.95%	

[1] Church memberships here given are taken from the 1964 *Yearbook of American Churches*, p. 252 and 280, published by the National Council of Churches of Christ in the U.S.A. These actually reflect 1963 totals and therefore vary slightly from later statistics supplied by the 1964 *Official Catholic Directory*.

[2] The "Etc." here means that Buddhists, Polish, Eastern Rite, and Old Catholics are included.

[3] This is the number in the *National Catholic Register*, Sept. 6, 1964, p. 5.

TABLE III—THE DEVELOPMENT OF RELIGIOUS DENOMINATIONS IN THE U.S.A.[1]

Denomination	1660	1740	1820	1860	1900	1950
Anglican-Episcopal	41	246	600	2,145	6,254	7,784
Baptist	4	96	2,700	12,150	49,905	77,090
Congregational	75	423	1,100	2,234	5,604	5,679
Dutch Reformed	13	129	380	1,116	2,296	3,517
Lutheran	4	95	800	2,128	10,287	16,403
Presbyterian	5	150	1,700	6,406	15,452	13,200
Quakers			350	728	1,031	654
Unitarian-Universalists			350	928	1,255	758
Methodist			2,700	19,883	53,908	54,000
Disciples				2,100	10,298	7,769
Christian Scientist					504	3,040
Mormons					1,041	2,700
Adventists				136	?	2,712
Assemblies of God						5,950
Brethren						1,029
Jewish		5		30		4,000
Church of God						6,972
Church of God in Christ						3,307
Nazarenes						3,480
Ev. United Brethren						4,323
Church of Christ						14,500
Greek Archdiocese						320
Mennonite						1,211
Pentecostal						3,682
Roman Catholic Parishes	12	27	124	2,550	10,339	15,533
TOTALS	154	1,171	10,804	52,532	168,174	259,613

[1] Statistics in this table are taken from the *Historical Atlas of Religion in America* by Edwin S. Gausted, Harper and Row, 1962, pp. 160-61.

TABLE IV—DENOMINATIONS AND CHURCH BODIES

Denomination	No. of Bodies	No. of Churches	Membership
Buddhist	1	55	60,000
Old Catholic, Polish, Etc.	7	348	597,372
Eastern Rite	20	1,454	3,001,000
Jewish	1	4,079	5,509,000
Roman Catholic[2]	1	23,412	43,847,938
R. C. Parishes		17,445	
Protestants	222	289,892	64,929,941
TOTALS	252	319,240	117,946,002

[1] From the 1964 *Yearbook of American Churches,* published by the National Council of Churches of Christ, p. 252. This reflects the 1963 membership.
[2] Cf. TABLE VI.

TABLE V—POPULATION AND CHURCH COMMUNICANTS IN THE U.S.A.

Year	Population[1]	Communicants	Jewish	Rom. Catholic	Protestants Etc.
1785	3,600,000	1,200,000[2]	No Data	18,200	1,150,000
1890	62,900,000	20,612,806[3]	130,496	6,257,871	14,223,439
1906	85,430,000	32,936,445[4]	101,457[5]	12,079,142	20,287,742[6]
1916	101,900,000	41,926,854[7]	357,135	15,721,815	25,847,904
1936	128,180,000	55,807,366[8]	4,641,184	19,914,937	31,251,245
1964	185,783,493[9]	117,946,002[10]	5,509,000	44,847,371[11]	68,528,313[12]

[1] For 1785 Census, cf. the *Catholic Yearbook of 1928,* p. 111. For the census counts of other years, cf. *Statistical Abstract* of 1963, p. 5.

[2] This number is based on the assumption that 32.85% of the population were church communicants, which is the proportion given in the 1890 *Abstract of the Census,* p. 259.

[3] Statistics for 1890 are taken from the 1890 *Abstract of the Census, ib.*

[4] Statistics for 1906 are taken from the 1906 *Census of Religious Bodies,* I 25.

[5] Reports on Jewish churches were incomplete this year, which accounts for the reduced figure.

[6] This total does not include the Eastern Orthodox or Latter Day Saints congregations, which had a combined total of 387,253 members in 1906.

[7] Statistics for 1916 taken from the 1916 *Census of Religious Bodies,* I, 19-21.

[8] Statistics for 1936 from the 1936 *ib.,* I 86-97.

[9] This figure for the 1964 population is taken from the *Official Catholic Directory,* p. 1381.

[10] Cf. TABLE IV.

[11] This is the latest count given in the 1964 *Official Catholic Directory,* p. 1381.

[12] This figure includes all denominations except Jewish and Roman Catholic.

TABLE VI—GROWTH OF THE CATHOLIC CHURCH IN THE UNITED STATES[1]

Category	In 1891	1936	1946	1964
Communicants	8,579,966	20,735,189	24,402,124	44,847,371
Priests	8,778	31,108	38,908	57,328
Brothers			6,721	12,132
Sisters			139,218	180,015
Parishes	7,631	12,720	14,523	17,445
Churches	9,381	18,387	21,963	23,541
Seminaries	39	197	342	571
Seminarians	1,711	22,629	22,950	48,750
Colleges & Universities	123	196	211	295
Students	?	?	102,665	366,172
High Schools	624	1,809	2,413	2,458
Students	?	195,821	477,190	1,068,541
Elementary Schools	3,277	7,490	8,036	10,902
Pupils	665,328	2,212,260	2,141,813	4,556,616
Released Time Pupils	None	None	812,998	4,316,931
Total Students			3,451,735	10,374,336
Hospitals			692	803
Baptisms			792,987	1,446,301
Converts			87,340	123,986
Marriages			245,267	329,450

[1] All statistics in this table are taken from the official *Catholic Directory* for the year involved: 1891, pp. 494-5; 1936, p. 1013; 1946, p. 1168; and 1964, p. 1381.

TABLE VII—VALUE OF AMERICAN CHURCHES
AND PARSONAGES: 1850-1936

Year	All	Jewish	Roman Catholic	Protestant, Etc.
1850: No. Churches[1]	38,061	36	1,222	36,803
Total Value	$87,328,801	$418,600	$9,256,758	$77,653,443
% of All	100	.47	10.54	89.00
1870: No. Churches	72,459	189	4,127	68,143
Total Value	$354,483,581	$5,155,234	$60,985,566	$286,342,781
% of All	100	1.45	17.22	81.33
1890: No. Churches[2]	142,521	303	8,816	132,404
Total Value	$679,630,139	$9,754,275	$118,371,366	$551,504,498
% of All	100	1.43	17.42	81.15
1906: No. Churches[3]	210,418	1,152	12,472	196,092
Total Value	$1,257,575,867	$23,198,925	$292,638,787	$941,738,155
% of All	100	1.86	23.28	74.86
1916: No. Churches[4]	227,487	1,901	17,487	208,099
Total Value	$1,895,446,678	$31,176,726	$435,545,176	$1,428,724,776
% of All	100	1.64	22.95	75.41
1936: No. Churches[5]	199,302	3,728	18,409	177,165
Total Value	$3,756,437,777	$123,695,037	$891,435,725	$2,741;307;015
% of All	100	3.29	23.73	72.98

[1] Data for 1850 and 1870 from the 1916 *Census of Religious Bodies*, I 24.

[2] Data for 1890 from the 1890 *Abstract of the Census*, p. 259.

[3] Data for 1906 from the 1906 *Census of Religious Bodies*, I 25.

[4] Data for 1916 from the 1916 *ib.*, I 19-21.

[5] Data for 1936 from the 1936 *ib.*, I 98-103.

89

TABLE VIII—EDUCATIONAL SYSTEMS
IN THE UNITED STATES: 1890-1964

Item	1890	1936	1964
U.S. Population[1]	62,900,000	128,180,000	188,000,000
Catholic Communicants	6,257,871[2]	20,735,187[3]	44,847,371[4]
Including children	(8,300,000)	20,735,187	44,847,371
% of Population	9.99 and 13.13	16.09	23.85
U.S. Children 5-17	18,543,201[5]	30,475,677[6]	46,674,000[7]
In Public Schools	12,722,581[8]	25,531,333[9]	41,757,665[10]
In Catholic Schools	665,328[11]	2,408,081[12]	5,625,157[13]
% of All Children	3.6	7.9	12.05
Cath. Children 5-17	2,300,000[14]	4,970,000[14]	11,210,000[15]
% in Cath. Schools	28.9	48.2	50.2
College and University	(for 1890)	(for 1946)	(for 1964)
Students in U.S.	237,592[16]	2,659,021[17]	4,206,672[18]
Public	90,689[16]	1,354,902[17]	2,596,904[18]
Private	146,903[16]	1,170,853[17]	1,609,768[18]
Catholic		102,655[19]	366,172[20]
% Catholic		3.8	8.7

Public School Pupils Receiving Catholic Instruction under Released Time	4,316,931[20]
Total Pupils Receiving Daily Catholic Instruction	9,942,088[21]
% of All Catholic Children	88.8

[1] Cf. TABLE V. Figure for 1964 is an estimate.
[2] Cf. TABLES V and VI. This includes only those 9 and over. The number below in parentheses is an estimate which includes children. *The Official Catholic Directory* for 1891, gives the total number for that year as 8,579,966.
[3] Cf. 1936 *Official Catholic Directory*, p. 1013.
[4] Cf. the 1964 *ib.*, p. 1381.
[5] Cf. *Statistical Abstract*, 1935, p. 107.
[6] This number is obtained from *ib.* by averaging figures for 1930 and 1940.
[7] Cf. the 1963 *Statistical Abstract*, p. 116. This is for 1962, but is the latest available at time of writing.
[8] Cf. 1935 *Statistical Abstract*, p. 107.
[9] Cf. the 1956 *ib.*, p. 115.
[10] Cf. *Research Report*, NEA, *Estimates of School Statistics*, 1963-64, p. 8.
[11] Cf. 1891 *Catholic Directory*, p. 494-5.
[12] Cf. *ib.* for 1936, p. 1013.
[13] Cf. TABLE VI.
[14] These numbers are based upon the assumption that Catholic families average the same number of children as others in the population.
[15] Assuming that 25% of all Catholics are between 5 and 17.
[16] These statistics are for 1899 and are taken from the *Digest of Educational Statistics*, published 1962, by the U.S. Department of Health, Education, and Welfare.
[17] These figures from *ib.* are for 1946.
[18] These statistics are from *Fall Enrollment in Higher Education*, 1962, published by the Department of H. E. and W.
[19] Cf. TABLE VI.
[20] *Ib.*
[21] *Ib.*

TABLE IX—REAL ESTATE ASSESSMENTS IN BUFFALO[1]

Category	1954	% of All Taxable	1964	% of All Taxable
TOTAL TAXABLE	1,020,347,140	100	1,036,123,658	100
Total Exempt	293,788,940	28.8	458,371,012	44.2
U.S.	35,065,190		30,827,630	
N. Y. State	15,502,710		30,469,100	
Erie County	7,017,390		8,376,580	
Buffalo City	77,376,280		79,603,660	
Public Schools	40,332,670		51,056,330	
Private Schools	25,361,120		42,817,070	
Religious:				
Protestant	14,752,080		18,456,570	
Catholic	16,689,860		22,999,990	
Hebrew	1,018,330		997,490	
Clergymen	75,000		333,410	
Charitable, Etc.	5,852,950		9,475,970	
Libraries	1,154,510		5,151,960	
Hospitals	12,611,290		25,981,220	
Veterans Exemptions	10,566,720		18,737,360	
Municipal Housing	21,248,490		51,765,810	
Cemeteries	6,528,660		6,455,310	
Railroads			45,642,962	
Miscellaneous	2,635,690		9,222,590	

[1] All data in this and the following two tables taken directly from the tax-rolls of Buffalo.

TABLE X—PRIVATELY OWNED, TAX-EXEMPT PROPERTY IN BUFFALO[1]

TOTAL:	$108,613,240	% of All Taxable:	10.48
RATIO OF RELIGIOUS:	70.93%	RATIO OF SECULAR:	29.08%

Category	Religious	Secular
Churches, Parsonages, Etc.	$42,787,460	
Charities and Social Services	2,639,700	$6,836,270
Hospitals	8,932,790	17,048,430
Schools and Colleges	22,552,570	1,360,710
Cemeteries	122,730	6,332,580
TOTALS:	$77,035,250	$31,577,990

[1] This does not include railroads or exempt portions of veterans' homes.

TABLE XI—THE DISTRIBUTION OF RELIGIOUS PROPERTY IN BUFFALO

Total of Religious Property:					$77,035,250	
Percentage of All Taxable Property:					7.43	
Proportion of Tax-Exempt Property in TABLE X:					70.93%	

Category	Jewish	% of All	Protestant	% of All	R. Catholic	% of All
Charities	$811,460	1.05	$708,870	.92	$559,620	.73
Social Services	559,750	.73	None		None	
Educational	11,120	.014	315,070	.41	22,226,380	28.84
Hospitals			126,420	.16	8,806,370	11.43
Churches, Etc.	997,490	1.29	18,456,570	23.96	23,333,400	30.29
Cemeteries	3,910	.005	96,990	.12	22,830	.03
TOTALS	$2,383,730	3.09	$19,702,920	25.57	$54,948,600	71.32

TABLE XII—GROWTH OF THE CATHOLIC CHURCH IN BUFFALO

Item[1]	1891	1906	1936	1964
Population of Buffalo[2]	255,664	381,819	575,000	528,000
Catholics in Buffalo[3]	(108,000)	(156,398)	242,587	(200,000)[4]
Over 9 or 13[5]	(85,000)	126,398	182,505	(150,000)
Catholic Children	(23,000)	(30,000)	60,082	(50,000)
Population of Diocese[6]				1,762,704
Catholics in Diocese[7]	160,000	202,019	408,349	897,200
	(over 9)	(over 13)	(All)	(All)
Outside Buffalo	(52,000)	45,621	165,762	697,200
Parochial Schools in Buffalo[8]	24	37	71	68
Pupils	9,946	17,346	32,518	30,725
% of All Catholics	9.2	11.1	13.4	15.4
Other Cath. El. & Sec. Schls			3	20
Enrollment			2,996	11,606
Total Enrollment	9,946	17,346	35,514	42,321
Cath. College Enrollment				5,087
Total Buffalo Enrollment				47,408
% of Catholics Enrolled	9.2	11.1	14.6	23.7
Parochial Schools in Diocese	44	86	168	189
Students In Catholic Schools Outside the City	7,489	9,167	22,686	61,297
% of Catholics There	14.4	20.1	13.7	8.8
Total Diocesan Enrollment	17,435	27,512	58,200	108,705
% of All Catholics	10.9	13.6	14.3	12.1
Public Sch. Pupils Receiving Cath. Instruction under Released Time in Sch. Hours				92,586
Total under Cath. Instruction				201,291
% of All Catholics in Diocese				22.4
%of all Catholics of School Age				89.9

1 The years here given were chosen because the U.S. Department of Commerce conducted religious censuses in 1906, 1916, 1926, and 1936.

2 Population in 1891 is that given in census for 1890. That for 1906 is given in the 1906 *Census of Religious Bodies*, I 380. That for 1936 averages the 1930 and 1940 Census counts. That for 1964 is a close estimate.

3 Figures given in this line are for all Catholics. Figures in parentheses in this and the line below are estimates; others are official. In 1891 and 1906, "children" means those under nine; in 1936, they are those under thirteen. The figures given for 1891 are based upon the known proportion of Catholics then in Buffalo. The figures for 1906 are from the *ib. Census of Religious Bodies*, I 380, which gives the number of Catholics over nine. For 1936, the *ib. Census of Religious Bodies*, I 470-1, gives complete information, both for adults and children.

4 In order to obtain our estimate of the number of Catholics in Buffalo in 1964, two factors must be considered: first, the decline in total population; and, second, the much larger reduction in white inhabitants. In 1930, the city had 573,000 people, of whom 13,563 (cf. 15th Census, Vol. III, Part 2, Table 15, p. 288) were Negroes; in 1964, these were 532,000 and 70,904 (cf. 18th Census, Vol. I, Part 34, p. 102) respectively. Since the great majority of Catholics were of European ancestry and since these were reduced from 559,000 to 451,000, or by 19% between 1930 and 1960, we conclude that Catholics declined by nearly the same proportion, or from 242,587 in 1936 to about 200,000 in 1964.

5 Cf. explanation above, Note 3.

6 Cf. 1964 *Official Catholic Directory*, summary for Buffalo.

7 Figures in this line for 1891 and 1964 are taken from the *Catholic Directory* for those years; those for 1906 and 1936 are from the *Census of Religious Bodies*, II 611 and II 2 1538-1540 respectively.

8 All statistics in this line and in all those below are taken from the *Catholic Directory* for 1891 and 1906 and the *Official Catholic Directory* for 1936 and 1964.

TABLE XIII—COMPARATIVE RELIGIOUS DEVELOPMENT IN BUFFALO[1]

Denomination	1906	1936	1964
All Churches	254	330	282
Total Valuation	$11,276,964	$38,889,616	$77,035,250
Average Value	44,397	117,847	273,174
Membership[2]	195,302	378,425	(340,000)
Jewish Congregations	9	15	8
Total Valuation	$183,000	(1,000,000)[3]	2,383,730
% of Total	1.62	2.57	3.09
Average Value	20,333	(66,000)	297,966
Membership	618	21,000	19,200
% of Total	.31	5.76	5.64
Protestants, Etc.	195	238	200
Total Valuation	$6,249,220	(26,143,258)	19,702,920
% of Total	55.41	67.23	25.57
Average Value	32,047	(110,309)	98,515
Membership	68,289	108,158	120,800
% of Total	35.00	28.58	35.53
Cath. Parish Churches[4]	50	78	74
Total Valuation	$4,844,744	(11,746,358)	54,948,600
% of Total	42.96	30.20	71.32
Average Value	96,895	(150,594)	742,549
Membership	126,395	248,467	200,000
% of Total	64.71	65.66	58.82

[1] Statistics for 1906 from the 1906 *Census of Religious Bodies,* I 380-402, 418-20, and II 611; and those for 1936 from *ib.,* I 470-1 and 432-33. This last, however, gives only the total value for all churches in the city, which we break down as shown below in Note 3. Data for 1964 is from TABLES XI and XII. We note a slight discrepancy in the total number of Catholics given here for 1936 compared to that given in TABLE XIII. This is because the one statistic is taken from the *Census of Religious Bodies* and the other from the *Official Catholic Directory;* both of these were for the same year, but may have reflected counts made several months apart. All estimates are placed in parentheses.

[2] The figure given in this line for 1906 is taken from the 1906 *Census of Religious Bodies,* I 380; that for 1936 from the 1936 *ib.,* I 470; that for 1964 is obtained by reducing the number of church communicants by the same proportion as the population declined, and is, therefore, an estimate.

[3] The estimates of Jewish, Protestant, and Catholic property for 1936 is determined as follows: (a) since 60 per cent of all Catholics in the diocese were residents of Buffalo at that time and since the total of diocesan property was $19,577,264 (*Census of Religious Bodies,* 1936, II 2 1538-40), that in Buffalo would approximate the amount here shown. (b) The amount given for Jewish property is a loose estimate, based upon the development of the communion. (c) Protestant property is determined mathematically by subtracting the combined Jewish and Catholic from the official total of $38,869,616, as given in the *Census of Religious Bodies.* It must be emphasized, however, that even though exact sums are given here, they are simply approximations.

[4] It will be noted that there were more Catholic churches than parishes in Buffalo in 1906 and 1936. There are many Catholic churches throughout the country which do not serve parishes. In 1964 there were about 6,000 of these.

TABLE XIV—THE PUBLIC AND CATHOLIC
SCHOOL SYSTEM OF BUFFALO

Category	1891	1936	1960
All El. and Sec. Enrollment	48,328	119,186	109,990
Total School Assessments			$67,991,070
Number of Public Schools[1]	51	86	98
Total Enrollment	36,382	83,672	67,583
% of All in Buffalo	78.5	70.3	61.4
Assessed Valuation			$51,056,330[2]
% of School Valuation in Buffalo			75.08
Valuation per Pupil			$758
Cath. El. and Sec. Schools[3]	24	74	95[4]
Total Enrollment	9,946	35,514	42,407
% of All in Buffalo	21.5	29.7	38.6
Assessed Valuation[5]			$16,934,740
% of Total School Valuation			24.91
Valuation per Pupil			$399

[1] The statistics covering the Buffalo public schools are taken from the 1890-91, 1936-37, and 1959-60 *Annual Report of the Board of Education,* Buffalo, New York.

[2] Cf. TABLE IX.

[3] For statistics covering Catholic schools, cf. above, TABLE XII.

[4] Statistics for 1960-61, taken directly from the 1961 *Official Catholic Directory.*

[5] The assessment on Catholic educational property for 1963-64 is $22,226,380 (cf. TABLE XI), of which $5,291,440 is placed on Catholic colleges and universities, leaving $16,934,940 for the parochial and other elementary and secondary Catholic schools.

TABLE XV—REAL ESTATE ASSESSMENTS IN THE DISTRICT OF COLUMBIA[1]

Category	Valuation	% of All	
All:	$4,653,591,031	100	
Taxable	2,525,485,494	54.3	
Exempt	2,128,105,537	45.7	
Exempt:		% of Exempt	
Federal	1,491,881,236	70.10	32.0
District	231,518,788	10.87	5.0
Private	404,705,513	19.02	8.7
Private Exempt:		% of All	% of Private
Religious	131,551,270	6.20	32.5
Educational	102,306,795	4.80	25.3
Foreign Governments	33,198,153	1.55	8.2
Charitable	20,531,448	.97	5.1
Cemeteries	7,497,535	.35	1.8
Hospitals	49,205,669	2.31	12.2
Libraries	3,136,078	.15	.8
Miscellaneous	57,278,565	2.69	14.1

[1] All statistics in this and the following tables are taken directly from the tax-rolls of Washington, D.C.

TABLE XVI—PRIVATE, EXEMPT PROPERTY IN THE DISTRICT OF COLUMBIA (TOTAL: $404,705,513)

Category	Religious	% Relig.	% of All	Secular	% Secular	% of All
Churches, Parsonages, Parochial Schools, Relig. Houses, Etc.	$131,551,270	59.36	32.50			
Educational	59,663,684	26.87	17.74	$42,643,111	23.33	10.52
Foreign Government	585,409	.26	.13	32,612,744	17.84	8.15
Charitable	8,789,079	3.96	2.18	11,733,369	6.41	2.89
Cemeteries	3,810,109	1.71	.94	3,687,426	2.01	.91
Hospitals	17,514,857	7.87	4.33	31,690,812	17.33	7.81
Libraries				3,136,078	1.71	.78
Miscellaneous				57,278,565	31.33	14.12
TOTAL	**$221,923,408**	**100.00**	**54.84**	**$182,782,105**	**100.00**	**45.16**

TABLE XVII—THE DIVISION OF RELIGIOUS PROPERTY
IN WASHINGTON
(TOTAL: $221,923,408)

Category	Jewish	%	Protestant	%	Catholic	%
Churches, Etc.	$4,970,343	2.25	$74,894,784	33.74	$51,687,143	23.29
Omitting National Shrines			58,523,484		40,656,582	
Churches & Schools Only					24,677,902	
Convents, Monasteries, Etc.					15,978,680	
Other Educational	517,865	.23	9,028,290	4.07	50,117,529	22.58
Foreign Government					585,409	.26
Charitable	1,562,383	.70	3,691,874	1.66	3,543,822	1.60
Cemeteries	316,422	.14	998,153	.45	2,495,534	1.12
Hospitals			2,134,214	.96	15,380,643	6.93
TOTALS	**$7,367,013**	**3.31**	**90,747,315**	**40.89**	**123,809,080**	**55.79**
WITHOUT THE NATIONAL SHRINES			$74,376,015		$112,779,519	

(These are the sums to be used for Extrapolation)

TABLE XVIII—COMPARATIVE DENOMINATIONAL DEVELOPMENT
IN WASHINGTON, D.C.

Denomination	1906[1]	1936[2]	1964[3]
Population[4]	307,000	560,000	760,000
All Churches	289	460	379
Total Valuation	$10,025,122	33,611,530	221,923,408
Average Value	$34,689	73,068	585,549
Communicants	136,759	271,724	350,500[5]
% of Population	44.5	48.52	46.11
Jewish Congregations	4	15	12
Total Valuation	$210,000	607,980	7,367,013
% of Total Value	2.09	1.80	3.31
Average Value	$52,500	40,532	613,751
Membership	698	18,350	45,000
% of Communicants	.52	6.75	12.8
% of Population	.23	3.28	5.8
Protestant Churches, Etc.	274	410	328
Total Valuation	$8,555,572	27,414,495	90,747,315
% of Total Value	85.35	81.58	40.88
Average Value	$31,224	66,621	276,670
Membership	92,283	172,684	225,000
% of Communicants	67.59	63.5	64.2
% of Population	30.06	30.8	29.6
Catholic Churches	21	35	39
Total Valuation	$1,259,550	5,588,058	123,809,080
% of Total Value	12.55	16.62	55.77
Average Value	$59,979	159,659	3,148,951
Membership	43,788	80,690	80,500
% of Communicants	32.39	29.6	23.0
% of Population	14.23	14.4	10.6

[1] Data for 1906 taken from the 1906 *Census of Religious Bodies*, I 172-5.

[2] Data for 1936 from 1936 *ib.*, I 188-92.

[3] Data for 1964 valuations are taken from TABLE XVII.

[4] The figures given for population for 1906, as well as for 1936, are derived from the official census by adding 60% of the ten-year increase to the number at the beginning of the decade.

[5] The statistics for 1964 giving the number of church communicants are derived from the *Study of Metropolitan Areas*, Series D, and from Bulletin, Series C, published by the National Council of the Churches of Christ in the U.S.A., both reflecting the situation as it existed in 1953-4. Necessary adjustments are made for the population changes between 1953 and 1964, both in number and in social type. The District lost 28,000 inhabitants between 1950 and 1960; 172,600 white people, or 30%, left during this period, while Negroes increased by 131,000; between 1946 and 1960, they increased by 224,000, and made up 54% of the population at the latter date, when they numbered 411,732 (cf. *Statistical Abstract*, 1963, p. 30). During the same time, the white population declined by 139,000. In 1953-4, there were 60,000 Jews, 109,140 Catholics, and 205,075 Protestants in the District. We assume that while Jews and Catholics lost about 25% of their membership, Negro Protestants more than replaced white members of that faith who left the city. Our estimate of 80,500 Catholics may be somewhat high, since this would be a decline of only about 18%; our estimate of Protestants may be too low, since nationally in 1953 75% of all Negroes were Baptists or Methodists; our estimate of Jews should be very nearly correct.

TABLE XIX—ENROLLMENT IN PUBLIC AND CATHOLIC SCHOOLS IN WASHINGTON

School System	1960[1]	% of All	% of Kind	1963[2]	% of Loss
Total Enrollment	136,517	100			
Catholic Total	23,517	17.2		18,760	20.2
Elementary	17,278	12.7	15.1	13,423	22.3
Secondary	6,239	4.5	19.4	5,337	14.6
Public Total	113,000	82.8			
Elementary	97,000	71.1	84.9		
Secondary	26,000	11.7	80.6		

[1] Statistics for 1960 public school enrollment taken from 1963 *Statistical Abstract*, p. 128. Statistics for 1960 Catholic enrollment are taken from the *Summary of Catholic Education*, 1960 and 1961, published by the National Catholic Welfare Conference, pp. 38 and 44.

[2] Statistics for 1963 are taken from the 1963 *Official Catholic Directory*, pp. 282-291.

TABLE XX—REAL ESTATE ASSESSMENTS IN BALTIMORE[1]

Classification	1964 Basis	% of
Total Taxable	$2,006,208,768	Taxable
Total Exempt	578,997,400	28.86

Exempt Categories:
1. Federal	22,667,510
2. State	25,671,480
3. City (Including Public Schools)	249,266,000
4. Churches, Synagogues, Parsonages, Church Related Schools, Etc.	89,430,950[2]
5. Colleges, Universities, Etc.	33,142,610
6. Cemeteries	4,577,530[3]
7. Lodges and Cultural Societies	7,858,110[4]
8. Hospitals, Dispensaries, Infirmaries	43,216,020
9. Wholesale Produce Market	552,400
10. Railroads	16,539,770
11. Housing Authority	39,284,940
12. Homes and Asylums	17,393,720
13. Miscellaneous	8,060,970
14. Market Authority	4,212,260
15. Blind Persons	1,124,790
16. Maryland Port Authority	15,997,840

[1] From the 1964 *Annual Report of Department of Assessments*, pp. 9 and 11.

[2] This category includes all parochial schools, as well as diocesan and private denominational institutions below college level, but no seminaries or specifically theological or religious academies, which are included under Category 5. It does, however, include a number of religious residences, as well as properties housing administrative and other ecclesiastical agencies.

[3] Although more than half the cemeteries are non-sectarian, there are quite a number of Protestant (mostly Lutheran), Catholic, and especially Jewish burial grounds in Baltimore.

[4] Most of the properties in this Category are secular.

99

TABLE XXI—EXEMPT SECULAR AND RELIGIOUS PROPERTY IN BALTIMORE[1]

Category	All	Religious	%	Secular	%
No. 4 Churches, Etc.	$89,430,950	89,430,950			
No. 5 Colleges, Etc.	33,142,610	9,552,870		23,589,740	
No. 6 Cemeteries	4,577,530	2,029,560		2,547,970	
No. 7 Lodges, Etc.	7,858,110	2,178,190		5,679,920	
No. 8 Hospitals, Etc.	43,216,020	19,648,480		23,567,540	
No. 12 Homes and Asylums	17,393,720	16,377,740		1,015,980	
No. 13 Miscellaneous	8,060,970	5,001,500		3,059,470	
TOTALS	**$203,679,910**	**144,219,290**	**70.81**	**59,460,620**	**29.19**

[1] Statistics in this and the following table are taken directly from the Baltimore tax-rolls. The reorganization of this data is our own.

TABLE XXII—THE DIVISION OF RELIGIOUS PROPERTY IN BALTIMORE
(TOTAL ASSESSED VALUATION: $144,219,290)

Category	Jewish	%	Protestant	%	Catholic	%
No. 4 Churches, Etc.	7,416,360	5.14	34,661,780	24.03	47,362,810	32.83
No. 5: Colleges, Etc.	881,860	.61	786,060	.55	7,884,950	5.47
No. 6: Cemeteries	1,190,940	.83	138,050	.10	700,570	.49
No. 7: Charities, Etc.	175,040	.12	1,076,640	.75	926,510	.64
No. 8: Hospitals, Etc.	56,940	.04	7,267,560	5.04	12,323,980	8.55
No. 12: Homes, Etc.	11,096,940	7.69	608,400	.42	4,672,400	3.24
No. 13: Miscellaneous	3,833,480	2.66	1,010,600	.70	157,420	.11
TOTALS	**$24,651,560**	**17.09**	**45,549,090**	**31.59**	**74,018,640**	**51.33**

TABLE XXIII—COMPARATIVE RELIGIOUS DEVELOPMENT
IN BALTIMORE[1]

Denomination	1906[2]	1936[3]	1964[4]
Population[5]	539,469	848,196	939,024
All Churches	443	544	619
Total Valuation	$15,198,810	32,571,060	144,219,390
Average Value	$34,309	59,873	232,987
Total Membership	(270,000)	434,720	(516,000)
Over 9 or 13	224,968	309,852	(390,000)
% of Population	50.05	51.26	54.97
Jewish Congregations	2	59	40
Total Valuation	$10,000	(3,600,000)	24,651,660
Average Value	$5,000	(61,017)	616,291
% of Total	.066	11.05	17.09
Membership	75	73,000	(66,000)
Over 9 or 13		(55,000)	(50,000)
% of Population	.011	8.73	7.03
% of Communicants	.03	16.79	12.79
Protestants, Etc.	400	424	509
Total Valuation	$12,204,010	(18,939,008)	45,549,090
Average Value	$30,510	(44,667)	89,487
% of Total	80.29	58.15	31.59
Total Membership	(147,725)	172,313	(250,000)
Over 9 or 13	124,496	129,511	(190,000)
% of Population	27.40	20.20	26.64
% of Communicants	54.71	39.65	48.45
Catholic Parishes	41	61	70
Total Valuation	$2,984,800	(10,032,052)	74,018,640
Average Value	$72,800	(164,460)	1,057,409
% of Total Value	19.64	30.80	51.32
Total Membership	(122,200)	189,407	(200,000)
Over 9 or 13	100,397	125,341	(150,000)
% of Population	22.64	22.34	21.30
% of Communicants	45.26	43.56	38.76

[1] All figures in parentheses are estimates; others are official.

[2] Data for 1906 taken from 1906 *Census of Religious Bodies*, I 412-15. Total church membership over 9 years of age only is given here.

[3] The 1936 *Census of Religious Bodies*, I 455-6, gives complete information concerning communicants, classing those under 13 as children. Concerning church holdings we are told only, *ib.* I 428, that total church property in Baltimore was $32,571,060. Since Catholics there (189,407) constituted 53% of those in the diocese at that time (349,225), *ib.* II 1530-40), we assume that the diocesan Catholic wealth ($18,928,437), *ib.*, was proportional, which would make it $10,032,050, which, of course, is only an approximation of that in Baltimore.

[4] For financial statistics under 1964, cf. TABLES XXI and XXII. For a discussion of how 1964 church membership is estimated, cf. text, Chapter IV. We should add that, according to the study of *Churches and Church Membership*, Series D. No. 1, published by the National Council of the Churches of Christ in the U.S.A., there were in Baltimore in 1950, 393 Protestant Churches (a decline of 31 from 1936) with 203,837 communicants. Between 1950 and 1960, therefore, 116 new Protestant churches came into existence with a probable membership of at least

101

40,000. We know that between 1950 and 1960, the white population declined by 111,000 and the Negro increased by 100,000. Since about 75% of the latter are Protestants, we add about 45,000 to the Protestant total. We reduce the Jewish membership by about 10% under the 1936 count. To estimate the Catholic membership in Baltimore is more difficult: there were almost 190,000 in 1936; nevertheless, since the Catholic percentage of the American population increased from 15.53 to 23.57% between 1936 and 1964, we estimate the number of Catholics in Baltimore roughly at 200,000 at the latter date.

[5] Population for 1906 from 1906 *Census of Religious Bodies,* I 380; that for 1936, by pro-rating that for 1930 and 1940; that for 1964 is the official count for 1960.

TABLE XXIV—RELIGIOUS PROPERTY IN BALTIMORE
IN TERMS OF 1936 DOLLARS
(Allowing for an Inflation of 150%)

Properties of Churches	Per Capita Wealth 1906	1936	1964 Valuations in 1936 Dollars	1964 Per Capita Wealth in 1936 $	In 1964 $
Protestant	$82	$110	$18,219,636	$73	$182
Jewish	133	49	9,860,664	149	374
Catholic	24	53	29,607,456	148	370

TABLE XXV—SECULAR AND CATHOLIC EDUCATION IN BALTIMORE

Item	1906	1936	1964
All Church Communicants[1]	224,968	434,720	516,000
Catholics in Baltimore[2]	(120,000)	187,407	(200,000)
Parishes in Baltimore[3]	41	61	70
Parochial Schools[4]	45	54	56
Enrollment	13,899	29,760	30,967
Other Catholic Schools, El. & Sec.[5]	10	10	11
Enrollment	1,300	2,900	8,508
Total Catholic City Enrollment	15,199	32,660	39,475
% of all Catholics	12.6	17.4	19.74
Colleges and Seminaries in City	2	2	5
Enrollment	185	195	4,375
Total City Enrollment of Catholics	15,384	32,855	43,850
% of All Catholics	12.8	17.6	21.93
Catholics in Whole Diocese[6]	250,000	349,226	429,403
Parochial Schools in Diocese[7]	95	138	107
Other Catholic Schools	25	36	64
Enrollment	4,563	14,528	22,377
Total Diocesan Enrollment	26,274	66,603	82,685
% of All Catholics in Diocese	10.5	18.9	19.3
Pupils in City Public Elementary and Secondary Schools[8]	61,977	117,546	175,037
In Secular Colleges and Universities[9]			16,862
Total			191,899
% of All Non-Catholics in City			25.9
Total in City El. & Sec. Schools	77,977	150,206	214,521
% Catholic	19.70	21.74	18.40
% Secular	80.30	78.26	81.60
Ratio of Total to Population	14.30%	15.4%	22.9%
Total in City Higher Education			21,235
% Catholic			20.59
% Secular			79.41
Public School Pupils Receiving Catholic Instruction under Released Time Arrangement[10]			17,253
Total Receiving Catholic Instruction[11]			99,938
% in Full-Time Sectarian Schools			83
% of All Catholics Receiving Sectarian Instruction			23.3

[1] Cf. TABLE XXIII.

[2] Cf. *ib.*

[3] As given for each year covered in the *Catholic Directory*.

[4] For statistics in this and the following line, cf. the 1906 *Catholic Directory*, p. 22; and the *Official Catholic Directory* for 1936 and 1964.

[5] The data for this and the following three lines for 1906 and 1936 are based on the assumption that since 48 and 54% of the Catholics in the diocese were in Baltimore at those two dates respectively, the secondary schools there would have a similarly correlational attendance. Cf. the 1906 *Catholic Directory*, p. 22, and

the *Official Catholic Directory*, 1936, p. 24. The data for 1964 is taken from *ib.* for 1964, pp. 17-24.

[6] The number given in this line for 1964 no longer includes the District of Columbia and several Maryland counties, which now make up the Washington archdiocese. Statistics for 1906 are taken from the *Catholic Directory*, published by M. H. Wiltzius Co. in 1906 and those for 1936 and 1964 from the *Official Catholic Directory* published by P. J. Kenedy and Sons Publishing Co. for those years.

[7] Statistics in this and the two following lines are taken from *ib.* for 1906, 1936, and 1964.

[8] Statistics covering Baltimore public school enrollment are taken from the *Annual Report of the Commissioners of Public Schools in Baltimore* for 1906, pp. 103 and 104; and from *ib.* for 1961, p. 4.

[9] This total obtained from data supplied in the 1964 *World Almanac*, pp. 513-26.

[10] Cf. the 1964 *Official Catholic Directory*, pp. 17-24.

[11] *Ib.*

TABLE XXVI—TAX-EXEMPT REAL PROPERTY IN DENVER
FEB. 1, 1963[1]

United States Government	$42,432,500
State of Colorado	17,991,430
City and County of Denver	43,588,040
Housing Authority	9,069,440
Public Schools	38,177,130
Colorado Seminary	8,347,170
Clayton Estate	1,584,070
Churches	19,609,310
Parochial Schools	8,479,070
Hospitals	11,519,350
Fraternal Organizations	2,489,170
Other Charitable Organizations	7,799,100
Private Schools	**3,519,770**
Parsonages	1,252,130
All Other	72,980
TOTAL	**$215,930,660**
TOTAL TAXABLE PROPERTY	**$1,169,942,550**
RATIO OF EXEMPT TO TAXABLE	**18.45%**

[1] All data in this and the three following tables consist of reports supplied by the assessor's office in Denver or are taken directly from the tax-rolls and organized or reorganized by ourselves.

TABLE XXVII—EXEMPT PRIVATE PROPERTY IN DENVER

Category	1962	1964
Colorado Seminary	$8,347,170	$12,426,200
Clayton Estate	1,584,070	1,498,030
Churches, Parsonages, Religious Houses, Church Schools, Etc.	29,340,510	31,177,880
Hospitals	11,519,350	16,302,080
Private Schools, Non Church	3,519,770	3,412,700
Fraternal, Charitable, and Other Non-Profit Organizations	10,361,250	13,065,580
TOTALS	**$64,672,120**	**$77,882,470**
TOTAL TAXABLE PROPERTY	**$1,169,972,120**	**1,152,398,040**
RATIO OF EXEMPT TO TAXABLE	**5.53%**	**6.75%**

TABLE XXVIII—SECULAR AND RELIGIOUS EXEMPT PROPERTY

Category	Total	Religious	Secular
Churches, Parsonages, Schools, Religious Houses, Etc.	$26,611,400	$26,611,400	
Other Schools and Seminaries	21,903,410	7,221,920	$14,681,490
Hospitals, Sanatoria, Etc.	16,302,080	12,724,240	3,577,840
Other Charitable and Non-Profit Properties	13,065,580	6,160,180	6,905,400
TOTALS	**$77,882,470**	**$52,717,740**	**$25,164,730**
%	**100**	**67.69**	**32.31**

THE DIVISION OF DENOMINATIONAL PROPERTY
(Total Assessed Valuation: $52,717,740)

Category	Jewish	%	Protestant	%	Catholic	%
Churches, Etc.	$1,150,770	2.18	15,640,010	29.67	8,364,590	15.87
Colleges, Etc.	364,960	.70	3,202,960	6.08	5,247,520	9.95
Hospitals, Etc.	4,918,960	9.32	3,910,270	7.42	5,098,990	9.67
Charities, Etc.	486,580	.92	273,470	.52	1,701,160	3.23
Apartments, Etc.	None		2,357,500	4.47	None	
TOTALS	**$6,921,270**	**13.12**	**25,384,210**	**48.16**	**20,412,260**	**38.72**

TABLE XXIX—COMPARATIVE RELIGIOUS DEVELOPMENT IN DENVER

Item	1906[1]	1936[2]	1964[3]
Population of City[4]	151,920	308,472	495,000
All Churches	175	223	395
Total Value	$3,610,050	$9,577,645	$52,717,740
Average Value	$20,629	$42,949	$133,463
Membership over 9 to 13	58,699	103,916	(207,000)
Including Children	(70,299)	142,906	(247,500)
% of Population	46.3	46.3	50.0
Jewish Congregations	10	16	10
Value of Property	$124,300	($800,000)	$6,921,270
% of All	3.44	8.35	13.13
Average Value	$12,430	($50,000)	$692,127
Membership over 9 to 13	703	(14,000)	(13,000)
Including Children		18,400	(17,000)
% of Communicants	1.0	12.9	6.8
% of Population	.46	6.0	3.4
Protestant Churches	152	182	347
Value of Property	$2,968,225	($6,552,645)	$25,384,210
% of All	82.22	68.41	48.14
Average Value	$19,528	($36,000)	$73,239
Membership over 9 or 13	32,003	59,329	(122,000)
Including Children	(38,404)	83,148	(140,500)
% of Communicants	54.6	58.1	56.8
% of Population	25.2	26.9	28.4
Catholic Parishes	13	25	38
Value of Property	$517,525	($2,225,000)	$20,412,260
% of All	14.34	23.23	38.72
Average Value	$39,809	($89,000)	$537,164
Membership over 9 or 13	25,993	26,187	(72,000)
Including Children	(31,192)	41,368	(90,000)
% of Communicants	44.4	28.9	36.4
% of Population	20.5	13.4	18.2

[1] Data for 1906 from *Census of Religious Bodies,* I 380-430 and 432-3.

[2] We have complete membership information for 1936, *Census of Religious Bodies,* I 499, but no breakdown of denominational property in individual cities—only the total for all: in this case, $9,577,645. However, the value of Catholic churches and parsonages in the diocese (cf. *ib.* II 1538-40) was $5,113,225; and since nearly 45% of the Catholics in the diocese lived in the Denver area, the proportional value was $2,225,000, which, of course, is an approximation. The $800,000 of Jewish religious property is a rough estimate.

[3] For financial figures under 1964, cf. TABLE XXVIII. Statistics for communicants are based upon *Bulletin* Series C, Number 1, p. 1, published by the National Council of Churches, reflecting the situation of 1953-54, according to which there were then in Denver 106,573 Protestants, 76,612 Catholics, and 16,000 Jews. Between 1953 and 1964, the population of Denver increased by at least 85,000, among whom 10,000 were Negroes. In making our estimates for 1964, we assume that approximately the same denominational proportions still obtain. All estimates are shown in parentheses.

[4] Population as given for 1906 is taken from the *Census of Religious Bodies,* I 380; those for 1936 are obtained by pro-rating the increase which took place during the decade. We add about 2,000 to the 1960 census count for our estimate of the 1964 population.

TABLE XXX—THE GROWTH OF THE CATHOLIC CHURCH IN DENVER[1]

Item	1891[2]	1906[3]	1936[4]	1964[5]
Population of the City	109,428	151,920	308,472	495,000
Communicants	(41,000)	85,830	142,916	(247,500)
Catholics	(20,000)	(31,192)	41,368	(90,000)
Over 9 or 13[6]		25,993	26,187	
% of Population	18.4	20.5	13.4	18.2
Catholic Parishes	8	13	25	38
With Schools	8	8	20	31
Enrollment	1,480	2,486	6,099	16,193
Other Cath. High Schools			2	5
Enrollment			188	1,767
Combined Enrollment	1,480	2,486	6,287	17,960
Pupils in Public Schools			47,306[7]	96,936[8]
Pupils in Public and Cath. Schools			53,593	104,896
% in Public Schools			88.8	84.3
% in Catholic Schools			11.2	15.7
Catholics in Diocese[9]				240,972
Population in Diocese				1,347,575
Ratio of Catholics				17.8%
Catholics in Sectarian Schools				31,256
Ratio to All Catholics				12.9%
Catholics in Public Schools Receiving Religious Instruction under Released Time				39,311
Total Pupils Receiving Catholic Instruction				70,569
Ratio to All Catholics				29.3%

[1] All figures shown in parentheses are estimates.

[2] Data for 1891 taken from the 1891 *Catholic Directory*, pp. 477-81.

[3] Data for 1906 taken from the 1906 *ib.* pp. 293-300.

[4] Data for 1936 taken from the 1936 *ib.* pp. 276-77.

[5] Data concerning Catholic school enrollment in the diocese taken from the 1964 *Official Catholic Directory*, pp. 79-83.

[6] The 1906 number is for persons over 9; that for 1936 for those over 13.

[7] There were 44,211 pupils in the elementary and secondary public schools of Denver in 1929-30; and since the population had increased by 7% in 1936, we add this percentage to the school enrollment to obtain the number here given. Cf. *Reports of Denver Public Schools*, Information Service Committee, 1930.

[8] Cf. *ib.*, dated April 30, 1964, published by the Denver Department of Education.

[9] For data in this and the following lines, cf. 1964 *Official Catholic Directory*, pp. 79-83.

TABLE XXXI[1]—COMPARATIVE RELIGIOUS DEVELOPMENT IN THE FOUR CITIES AND IN THE UNITED STATES

Denomination	1906	1936	1964
Population of U.S.[2]	85,400,000	128,181,000	186,000,000
Population of 4 Cities	1,254,033	2,222,614	2,722,000[3]
% of National	1.48	1.73	1.46
Number, U.S. Churches	210,418	199,302	319,240
In 4 Cities	1,167	1,557	1,674
% of Total	.55	.78	.52
Communicants in U.S.	32,936,445	55,807,366	117,946,002
In Average Church	157	285	370
% of Population	38.57	43.53	63.41
Jewish Communicants in U.S.	101,457	4,641,184	5,509,000
For Average Synagogue	881	1,245	1,350
% of All Communicants	.308	8.32	4.67
% of Population	.12	3.62	2.96
Protestants, Etc. in U.S.	20,755,846	31,251,456	68,589,065
In Average Church	106	176	236
% of All Communicants	63.02	56.00	58.17
% of Population	24.30	24.38	36.88
Catholics, in U.S.	12,079,142	19,914,937	43,847,937
In Average Parish	1,580	1,565	2,514
% of All Communicants	36.67	35.68	37.16
% of Population	14.14	15.53	23.57
Communicants in 4 Cities	671,840	1,227,785	1,453,500
In Average Congregation	574	788	868
% of Population	53.58	55.24	53.39
% of U.S. Communicants	2.04	2.22	1.23
Jewish Communicants in 4 Cities	2,094	131,550	147,200
For Average Synagogue	484	1,253	2,103
% Communicants in 4 Cities	.31	10.72	10.13
% of Population in 4 Cities	.17	5.92	5.41
% U.S. Jewish Communicants	2.06	2.83	2.67
Protestants, Etc., in 4 Cities	348,371	536,303	735,800
In Average Church	341	428	532
% Communicants in 4 Cities	51.85	43.69	50.62
% Population in 4 Cities	27.77	24.13	27.03
% U.S. Protestants	1.68	1.72	1.07
Catholics in 4 Cities	321,375	559,932	570,500
In Average Parish	2,571	2,828	2,593
% Communicants in 4 Cities	47.84	45.59	39.25
% Population in 4 Cities	25.63	25.20	20.95
% of U.S. Catholics	2.65	2.81	1.30

[1] All statistics given in this and the following tables are compilations of figures from previous tables, unless otherwise stated. Source citations are not repeated.
[2] The statistics for 1906 and 1936 population are taken from the 1963 *Statistical Abstract*, p. 5; the figure for 1964 is an estimate, which could vary as much as 2 million during the course of the year.
[3] The statistics for church communicants given under 1964 are from the 1964 *Yearbook of American Churches*, published by the National Council of Churches; this summarizes data for 1963. Because the 1964 *Official Catholic Directory* is based upon later information, it shows increases in all items. Finally, statistics released late in 1964 by the National Catholic Welfare Conference concerning fall enrollment in Catholic schools show another large increase over the summaries given in the 1964 *Official Catholic Directory*; these will probably appear in the 1965 edition of this work.

TABLE XXXII—ASSESSED VALUE OF RELIGIOUS PROPERTY IN FOUR CITIES AND IN THE UNITED STATES

Denomination	1906	1936	1964
Of All Churches in 4 Cities	$40,110,946	$114,849,054	$468,494,827
% of All Exempt			24.78
% of Private Exempt			58.66
% of National Religious	3.19	3.06	1.54
Average for Each Congregation	$34,371	$77,763	$280,463
Jewish Wealth in 4 Cities	$527,300	$6,007,980	$41,323,573
% of Wealth There	1.31	5.23	8.82
% of Jewish National Wealth	2.27	4.85	2.86
Synagogues There	25	105	70
Average Wealth	$21,092	$57,219	$590,336
Protestant Wealth 4 Cities	$29,977,027	$79,248,722	$165,012,235
% of Wealth There	74.74	69.00	35.22
% of Prot. Nat'l Wealth	3.18	2.89	1.47
Churches There	1,021	1,253	1,384
Average Wealth	$29,360	$62,449	$119,229
Wealth Per Capita	$86	$148	$224
Catholic Wealth in 4 Cities	$9,606,619	$29,592,352	$262,159,019
% of Wealth There	23.95	25.76	55.96
% of Cath. National Wealth	3.28	3.32	1.47
Parishes There	125	198	220
% of National	1.6	1.8	1.3
Average Wealth	77,741	$149,456	$1,191,178
Per Capita Wealth	$30	$53	$460
All U.S. Churches	$1,257,575,867	$3,756,437,777	($31,800,000,000)
Average Wealth	$5,988	$18,876	($99,700)
All Jewish Synagogues	$23,198,925	$123,695,037	($2,800,000,000)
% of National	1.84	3.29	(8.80)
No. Synagogues	1,152	3,728	4.079
Average Wealth	$20,138	$33,180	($686,000)
Protestant, Etc., Churches	$941,738,155	$2,741,307,015	($11,200,000,000)
% of National	74.91	72.98	(35.22)
No. Churches	196,418	177,165	289,899
Average Wealth	$4,805	$15,487	($38,630)
Wealth Per Capita	$45	$87	($163)
Catholic Wealth	$292,638,787	$891,435,725	($17,800,000,000)
% of National	23.25	23.73	(55.97)
No. Parishes	7,643	12,720	17,445
Average Wealth	$38,159	$70,080	($1,020,300)
Wealth Per Capita	$24	$45	($400)

TABLE XXXIII—THE CATHOLIC EDUCATIONAL SYSTEM IN THE UNITED STATES AND IN THE FOUR CITIES: ENROLLMENT

Category	Elementary and Secondary	Colleges and Universities
In U.S.	6,073,447	425,844
In Four Cities	118,506	23,358
% in Four Cities	1.95	5.48

TABLE XXXIV—ASSESSED AND ESTIMATED TRUE VALUATIONS OF PROPERTY IN THE FOUR CITIES AND IN THE UNITED STATES

Total Assessment in 4 Cities[1]	$10,109,164,079
Omitting District Federal Property	8,627,282,843
Total Exempt	3,381,404,609
Ratio to Total	33.41%
Total Exempt, Omitting District Federal	1,889,523,373
Ratio to Total	21.90%
Total Private Exempt	794,881,135
Ratio to Total, Omitting District Federal	9.22%
Total Religious Property	468,494,827
Ratio to Total, Omitting District Federal	5.46%

Estimated Private Exempt Property in the United States, as Assessed on the Tax Rolls	($54,000,000,000)
Estimated Assessed Value of All U.S. Property	($455,870,000,000)
Estimated True Value of This Property	(1,140,000,000,000)
Estimated True Value of Private Exempt Property in the U.S.	($135,000,000,000)
Ratio to Total	(11.8%)
Estimated Assessed Value of All Exempt Property (Excluding District Federal from Our Extrapolation, Which Makes Our Computation too Low, Since Every City Has a Considerable Corpus of such Property)	($130,000,000,000)
Estimated True Value of This Property	($325,000,000,000)
Ratio All U.S. Property	(28.5%)

[1] All sums given in this table cover only real estate and make no computation of personal or intangible property, nor of investments in streets, sidewalks, sewers, roads, etc., or of federal or state projects, such as dams, parks, etc.

NOTES

FOREWORD

1. *Christianity Today*, Oct. 13, 1961.
2. Cf. *Churches and Church Membership in the U.S.*, Series A, No. 2, published by the National Council of Churches.

CHAPTER I

1. *The Catholic Yearbook for 1928*, p. 111.
2. *Ib.*
3. *Ib.*
4. *Ib.*
5. *Ib.*
6. The official census.
7. *The Catholic Yearbook for 1928*, p. 113.
8. Cf. the 1925 *Statistical Abstract*, p. 85.
9. Page 113.
10. Cf. 1964 *World Almanac*, pp. 622-28.
11. Cf. TABLE IV.
12. Cf. 1925 *Statistical Abstract*, p. 85.
13. As shown in the *Official Catholic Directory* for that year, and on p. 1013 of the 1936 edition of the same publication.
14. Cf. the 1963 *Statistical Abstract*, p. 99. The 1924 law limits European immigrants to approximately 155,000 annually, of whom no more than 60,000 may come from predominantly Catholic countries.
15. *Abstract of the Census* for 1890, p. 259.
16. Cf. the 1906 *Census of Religious Bodies*, I 37.
17. Statistics for 1890 taken from the 1890 *Abstract of the Census*, p. 259.
18. Cf. the 1936 *Census of Religious Bodies*, I 87-97.
19. This figure is obtained by dividing the number of Protestant churches (289,892) into the number of communicants (64,929,941), as given in the 1964 *Yearbook of American Churches*, p. 252.
20. These figures are obtained by the same process, using the statistics given in TABLE VI.
21. Cf. the *Catholic Encyclopaedia*, Special Edition, 1913, XIII, pp. 580-1.
22. *Ib.*
23. *Ib.*
24. *Ib.*

25. *The National Catholic Register*, Sept. 6, 1964.
26. *Ib.*

CHAPTER II

1. As stated in the *National Catholic Register*, May 17, 1964; and as shown in the 1964 *Official Catholic Directory*, p. 358.
2. *Study of Metropolitan Areas in the United States*, Bulletin, Series D, No. 1, 1957, published by the National Council of Churches.
3. *Report of the Buffalo Department of Education*, 1890-91.
4. Cf. the Buffalo *Courier Express*, Nov. 27, 1960.

CHAPTER III

1. Cf. the 1890 *Abstract of the Census*, p. 259.
2. Cf. the 1960 *Official Catholic Directory*.
3. Cf. Note 5 under TABLE XVIII.
4. Cf. *Bulletin, Series D, No. 2*, in studies in *Churches and Church Membership in the U.S.*, published by the National Council of Churches.
5. Cf. 1964 *World Almanac*, p. 515 and p. 517.
6. Cf. article in the Washington *Post*, July 31, 1964.
7. Cf. Ch. VIII, Note 38.

CHAPTER IV

1. Cf. 1964 *Official Catholic Directory*, p. 17.
2. Cf. the 1936 *Annual Report of the Health Department of the City of Baltimore*, p. 248, and the *ib.*, 1960, p. 229.
3. Cf. the 1960 *ib.* p. 229. The white portion of the population declined from 685,000 in 1936 to 610,000 in 1960.
4. Cf. the 1964 *Official Catholic Directory*, pp. 17-24.
5. The July report of the Health Department of the City of Baltimore states that during the first six months of 1964 there were 4,682 white and 4,713 non-white births.
6. Cf. the 1964 *World Almanac*, pp. 513-26.

CHAPTER V

1. Cf. the *Rocky Mountain News*, Aug. 14, 1964.
2. Cf. *Churches and Church Membership in the U.S.*, Series D, No. 1, published by the National Council of Churches of Christ in the U.S.A.

CHAPTER VI

1. Cf. the 1964 *Yearbook of American Churches*, p. 286, published by the National Council of Churches.
2. Cf. the 1964 *Official Catholic Directory*, Summary.

CHAPTER VII

1. Cf. Genesis 47:22, 26.
2. Ezra 7:24.
3. Cf. the *Institutes of Vishnu*, III, 26-27; V 2, 8; *The Laws of Manu*, VII 133; *The Institutes of Gautama*, VIII 13, all published in *The Sacred Books of the East*, edited by Max Muller.
4. Cf. Eusebius, *Ecclesiastical History*, X v 15-20; vi, vii; and *The Life of Constantine*, III lxiv, lxvi, published in the *Nicene Fathers*.
5. *Internal Revenue Code*, Sec. 170 (a) (1) and (b) (1) (A) (B).
6. *Ib.* 119 (1) and (2).
7. *Ib.* Sec. 107 (a).
8. Cf. TABLES XV and XVI.
9. Cf. TABLES X and XI.
10. Cf. Ch. II and TABLE IX.
11. Cf. *Internal Revenue Code*, Sec. 511 (a) (2) (A).
12. In Sub-chapter F., Sec. 501 through Sec. 514.
13. Under Sections 501, 502, and 503 of the *Internal Revenue Code*.

CHAPTER VIII

1. *Christianity Today*, Aug. 3, 1959.
2. Cf. TABLE XV.
3. Article in the Buffalo *Express*, Nov. 27, 1960. Cf. also TABLE IX.
4. Cf. TABLE XX.
5. Cf. TABLE XXV.
6. Cf. TABLE XXXI.
7. Summary, p. 2.
8. *Wall Street Journal*, Oct. 29, 1963.
9. Cf. *Subcommittee Chairman's Report on Tax-Exempt Foundations*, Dec. 31, 1962; and Oct. 16, 1963, and March 20, 1964.
10. Cf. summary of Treasury Report published in the *Arizona Republic*, Feb. 8, 1965, p. 17.
11. *Ib.*
12. *Christianity Today*, Oct. 13, 1961.
13. *Wall Street Journal, ib.*, and *Christianity Today, ib.*
14. Highly publicized at the time.
15. *Wall Street Journal, ib.*, and *Christianity Today, ib.*
16. *Ib.*
17. *Wall Street Journal, ib.*
18. *Christianity Today, ib.*
19. *Ib.*
20. *Wall Street Journal, ib.*
21. *Ib.*
22. Cf. *Arizona Republic*, Oct. 22, 1964. Cf. deed in Maricopa County Records, 3796/122.
23. Oct. 29, 1963; cf. also *Christianity Today, ib.*
24. Oct. 29, 1963.
25. *Ib.*
26. Cf. TABLE XXXI.
27. *The Columbia Magazine*, Oct. 20, 1960.

28. *Wall Street Journal, ib.*
29. Cf. *The Milwaukee Journal,* Aug. 18, 1963.
30. Cf. *Christianity Today, ib.*
31. Cf. many articles in *Church and State,* published by Protestants and Others United, dealing with this case.
32. Sections 501 (b) ; 511 (a) (1) (2) (A) ; and 512 (a).
33. The information in this paragraph was compiled by the Research Department of POAU, August, 1961.
34. *Wall Street Journal, ib.*
35. Personal knowledge of writer.
36. Cf. *Church and State,* June, 1964, p. 12.
37. Cf. Ch. III, this study.
38. Cf. the elaborate brochure published by the Watergate Realty Company, which is promoting the sales and rentals of the project; also the full-page article in the Washington *Evening Star,* April 10, 1964.
39. Published April 30 and August 13, 1958.
40. January 1, 1962.

INDEX

American University, Methodist, 21
Anglicans, 3, 5
Apostolic Delegate of the Holy See, 21
Archer, Dr. Glenn, iv

Baltimore, a trading city, x; cf. pp. 27-33; had first Catholic episcopate, 27; founded by Lord Calvert, 27; distinguished by Johns Hopkins University and Hospital, 27; churches and synagogues, 27-28; Cathedral of Mary Our Queen, 28; exempt property, 28; secular, exempt properties, 28-29; religious properties, 29-30; denominational development, 30-32; Jewish growth, 30; church communicants, 30; Protestant development, 30-31; Catholic development, 30-32; denominational wealth, 33; real estate assessments, 101; exempt secular and religious property, 102; comparative religious development, 103; 1964 religious property in 1936 dollars, 104; secular and Catholic education, 105.
Bank of America, 76
Baptist Joint Committee, v
Baptists, 3, 5, 22, 55
Biltmore Hotel of Dayton, Ohio, 69
Bishop, Catholic, powers of, as a *corporation sole*, 57-58; living standard of, 58; immunity to taxation, 58-59
Blake, Dr. Eugene Carson, quoted, v, 65
Buddhists, ix
Buffalo, x; cf. pp. 11-17, social and religious complex, 10; property assessments, 10-11; privately owned, exempt real estate, 12-13; denominational properties, 13; construction of

parochial schools, 16; better Catholic schools in suburbs, 16; assessments on religious property minimized, 17; commercial and residential property heavily taxed, 17; estimated value of Catholic property, 18; real estate assessments, 1954 and 1964, 93; privately owned, exempt property, 94; growth of Catholic Church, 95; comparative religious development, 96; public and Catholic school systems, 97
Business income, of all non-profit entities should be taxed, 82

Canisius High School and College in Buffalo, 17-18
Carroll, Bishop John, founded Georgetown University, 4
Cathedral of Mary Our Queen, in Baltimore, 28; assessments on, 28
Catholic Church, growth in Roman Empire and in U.S., xiii; conflict and persecution, xiv; privileges and immunities under Constantine, xiv; slow American growth, 3; in New Mexico and Florida, 3; established in Maryland, 3; in New York, 4; growth by immigration, 4; attitude toward religion in public schools, 5; vast complex of facilities, 6; huge immigration, 7; losses, 7; growth of property, 7-8; size of congregations, 8; education, 8; decrees concerning schools, 9; growth in membership, 8-10; community value of educational system, 10; expansion in Buffalo, 13-15; schools in Buffalo, 13-15; value

115